Blender 2.8 for architecture

Modeling and rendering with Eevee and Cycles

I0002729

Allan Brito

Description and data

Technical info about the Book

Author: Allan Brito

Reference: blender3darchitect.com

Edition: 1st (Revision 3)

Cover image credits: Samuel Zeller @Unsplash

Licensed in public domain - https://unsplash.com/license

Blender version used in the Book: 2.80

First edition date: July 2019

ISBN: 9781086438437

Imprint: Independently published

About the author

Allan Brito is a Brazilian architect that has a passion for applying technology and open source to design and visualization. He is a longtime Blender user ever since 2005, and believes the software can become a great player in the architecture and design markets.

You will find more about him and the use of Blender for architecture in **blender3darchitect.com**, where he writes articles about the subject on a daily basis.

Who should read this book?

The book has a goal of guiding artists looking to start using Blender 2.8 for architectural visualization. No matter if you already know Blender. We will start from the very beginning.

You don't need any previous experience with Blender to follow the chapters.

Foreword

The release of Blender 2.8 is a milestone for every artist that uses Blender as a tool to create digital art, and for architectural visualization artists, it brings a lot of new options.

One of the highlights of Blender 2.8 for architecture is the debut of Eevee, which has the potential to disrupt the way you work with architectural visualization. With Eevee, you can create realistic images in a matter of seconds instead of hours. You don't even need the latest hardware to get that performance.

A real-time render engine like Eevee is a game-changer for Blender regarding architectural visualization. What if you still need photorealistic images? You can still use Cycles that have a robust algorithm to produce realistic images.

A benefit of having two engines integrated to Blender 2.8 is that they share a lot of settings like materials. You have to do the setup for just one of them.

The purpose of this book is to explain and demonstrate how you can use Blender 2.8 for architecture with examples and techniques related to modeling, texturing, and rendering.

Since our focus is with the architecture, we also deal with aspects of this type of production like importing CAD data, handling furniture models, and precision modeling.

If you want to work with Blender and produce content related to architecture, you will find a lot of useful information in this book.

I hope you enjoy the content and that by the end you can start using Eevee and Cycles to produce beautiful images for your designs.

Allan Brito

Downloading Blender

One of the significant advantages of Blender when comparing to similar softwares is their open source nature. You can use Blender without any hidden costs! All you have to do is download the software and start using it.

How to download it? To download Blender, you should visit the Blender Foundation website:

https://www.blender.org/download/

For this book, we will use version *2.80 of Blender*, but the vast majority of techniques will still work with later versions.

Intentionally left blank

TABLE OF CONTENTS

Chapter 1 - Blender for architecture

With the release of Blender 2.8 and some of their new features like Eevee, a significant amount of artists will try the software for the first time. A typical step for everyone trying to begin working with Blender is to learn how the user interface works.

The user interface is much more friendly in Blender 2.8, and you will find lots of options regarding architectural design, like precision modeling and real-time render engines.

In this chapter, we will focus on the interface. Here is what you will learn:

- Interface manipulation and Workspaces
- Keyboard shortcuts and Editors
- 3D Navigation
- Object selection
- 3D Transformations
- Object creation
- 3D Cursor and Snap
- Work modes
- Saving projects

1.1 Blender basics for architecture

The first thing you must learn before starting using Blender for architecture is their user interface. The interface has some unique features to help you work faster in 3D. When you open Blender for the first time, you will see the default user interface (Figure 1.1).

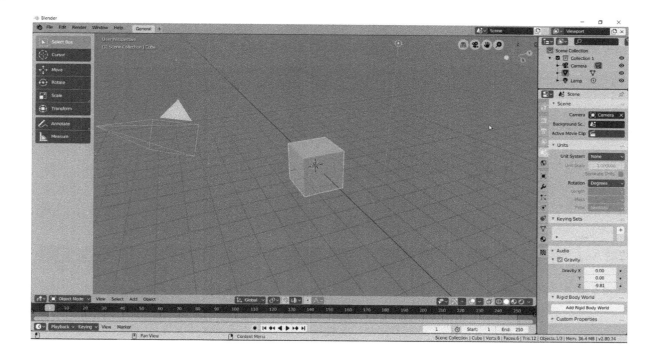

Figure 1.1 - *Default user interface*

Why is that the default user interface? Because you will learn later that this interface arrangement can change in any way you like.

One of the core concepts of the Blender user interface is the use of divisions called editors. Each editor has a specific purpose and will contribute to an architectural project in different ways.

You can change the editor type by using the selector available at the header of each division (Figure 1.2).

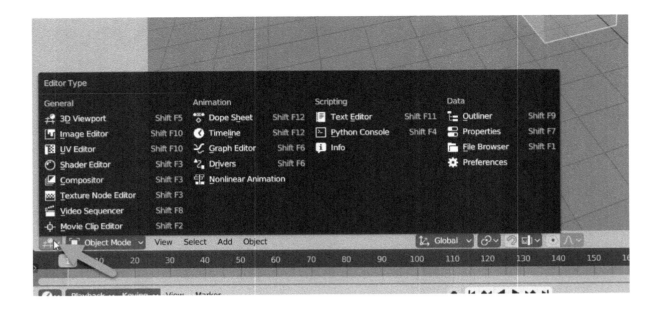

Figure 1.2 - Editor selector

In each editor, you will find a header that shows you some menus, tools, and options related to that specific editor. The default user interface will show us with the following editors:

– **3D Viewport**: The place where you will see all 3D modeling and scene setup.

– **Outliner**: An editor that helps you organize the scene in collections.

– **Properties**: One of the most important editors, because it shows options related to each selected object that allows you to change and manipulate each object.

– **Timeline**: If you have plans to work with animation, you will be able to control timing and interpolation in this editor.

Another feature of some editors is the availability of tabs on the sides of each editor. Not all of them will feature a tab with additional options, but one that has two tabs is the 3D Viewport.

The Toolbar on the left shows several icons and options related to object manipulation and modeling. You can toggle this tab using the T key. On the right side, we have the Properties tab. That will show options related to selected objects and the 3D Viewport. The N key will open and close this tab (Figure 1.3).

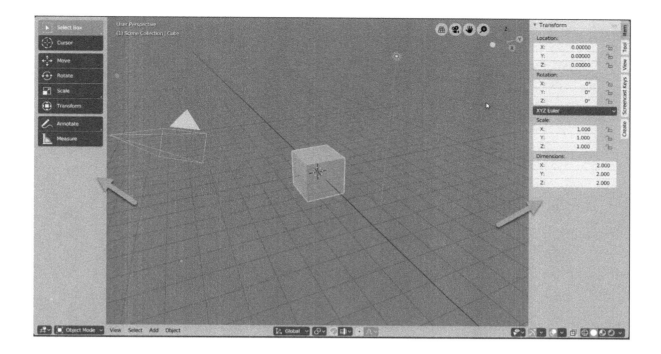

Figure 1.3 - *Tabs in the 3D Viewport*

Other editors will also feature those tabs with different purposes and options.

1.1.1 Interface divisions

One of the fundamental aspects of the Blender user interface is the ability to make divisions and resize editor in any way you need. If you want to resize an existing editor, you can place the mouse cursor at the line marking the division between two editors. When you do that, the cursor will turn into a double side arrow.

At this moment, you can click and drag to resize the editor (Figure 1.4).

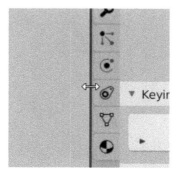

Figure 1.4 - *Resizing editors*

Besides resizing editors, you can also make new divisions with a right-click at the same border between two existing editors. When you click at the edge, a small menu called "Area Options" will appear (Figure 1.5).

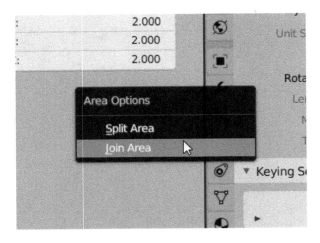

Figure 1.5 - *Area Options*

If you choose the Split Area, you will make a new division at the interface, and with the Join Area, you can merge two existing editors.

You have to follow two simple rules to use the Area Options:

- **For divisions**: You will always have a division in the opposite direction of the border you choose. For instance, if you select a vertical edge, you will get a horizontal division.

- **For join editors**: Both editors must share the same border in size to join.

There are other options to manage interface divisions at the **View** → **Area** menu. For instance, there you will find the "Toggle Quad View" to quickly make four divisions to the 3D Viewport (Figure 1.6).

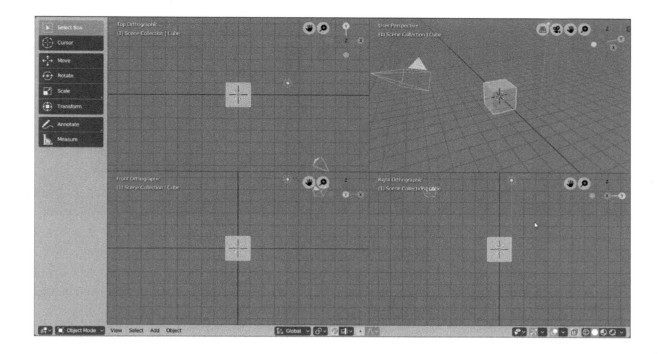

Figure 1.6 - *Quad view*

Each division will feature an orthographic view to help you work with 3D Modeling.

Another important option in this menu is the "Duplicate Area into New Window." It will allow you to get an editor in Blender and detach it from the user interface to a new window.

If you plan to use multiple monitors with Blender, you can make multiple instances of editors utilizing that option.

1.1.2 Workspaces

What are Workspaces? That is how Blender calls an interface template that has all the necessary editor ready to perform a specific task. The Workspace selector is at the top of the interface with multiple arrangements available.

If you click at the "+" button, you will see a list with all the existing templates by category (Figure 1.7).

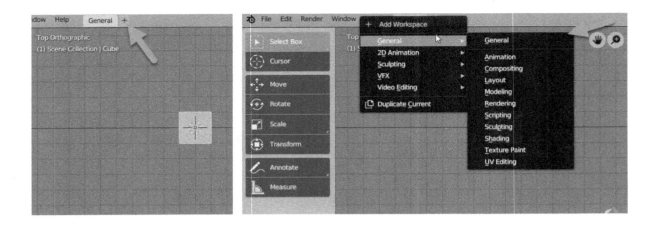

Figure 1.7 - *Workspace templates*

For instance, if you get the Modeling option from the General group, you will get all editors related to animation removed and only tools for modeling available (Figure 1.8).

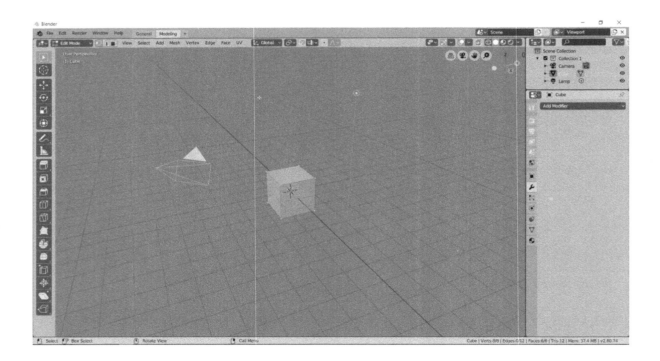

Figure 1.8 - *Modeling Workspace*

You can even rename a Workspace with a double-click on their name. That is a great way to keep your interface template organized, and you can also reuse that layout on other projects.

1.1.3 Active editor and shortcuts

An important concept regarding editors and the user interface in Blender is the active editor. You will find that Blender uses a lot of keyboard shortcuts to offer artists a way to call a tool or navigate in 3D quickly.

No matter what you want to do in Blender, you probably will find a keyboard shortcut that will help you perform a task. When you press the key for that shortcut Blender will call the tool using the active editor you have at the moment.

The active editor will always be the one you have the mouse cursor. For instance, if you place the cursor at the Viewport and press a key. Blender will apply the shortcut to that specific editor.

That is important for tasks like 3D modeling because most of the work will happen at the Viewport editor. If you press the shortcut keys on any other editor, they won't work.

1.2 Shortcuts and 3D navigation

If you have plans to start using Blender to create 3D models and render projects for architecture, you must learn how to navigate in 3D first. Every tool or software have their collection of shortcuts and methods to handle 3D space.

Blender is no different, and you will find several unique options to handle Navigation. Most of the Navigation-related shortcuts will require you yo have the mouse cursor at the Viewport, or any other editor you wish to manipulate.

Here is a list with the main shortcuts for 3D navigation in Blender:

- **SHIFT+Middle mouse button (Wheel)**: Move the screen

- **CTRL+Middle mouse button (Wheel)**: Zoom in and out

- **Mouse Wheel**: Zoom in and out

- **Middle Mouse Button**: Orbit the 3D scene

- **+ and - keys**: Zoom in and out

- **Numpad 5**: Change projection from perspective to orthogonal

- **Numpad 1**: Front view

- **Numpad 3**: Right view

- **Numpad 7**: Top view

- **Numpad 0**: Camera view

- **CTRL+ Numpad 1, 3, or 7**: Opposite view

- **Home key**: Zoom all

All shortcuts will work on multiple editors to keep consistency. If the editor you are using doesn't have 3D data to show, you won't be able to use navigation shortcuts like the orthographic views or 3D Orbit.

As you can see from the list, it is essential to have a keyboard with a Numpad available. What if you are using a keyboard that doesn't have a Numpad? For those cases, you can emulate the Numpad using the **Edit → Preferences...** menu and at the Input tab, choose the Emulate Numpad option (Figure 1.9).

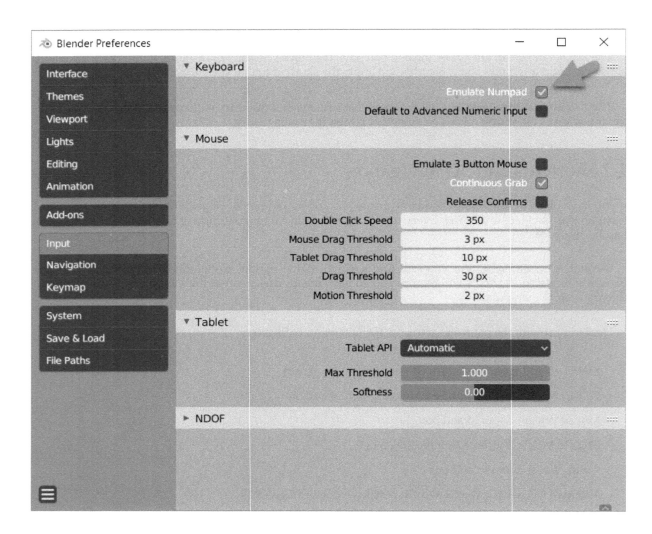

Figure 1.9 - *Emulate Numpad*

There are also other options for viewing scenes in 3D that are available at the View menu on each editor.

1.2.1 Navigation widgets

The use of shortcuts is essential to enabling a quick 3D navigation in Blender. But, it doesn't mean you don't have options to manipulate the way you view your projects using only the mouse.

With the navigation widgets on the top right of your Viewport, you have much of the options from the shortcuts, with the convenience of using only the mouse (Figure 1.10).

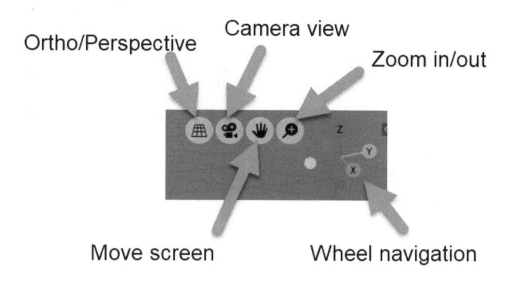

Figure 1.10 - Navigation Widget

The navigation wheel will allow you to change several aspects of your viewing:

– Click and drag inside the circle to start a 3D Orbit

– Click on any circle with the axis as a label to trigger an orthographic view

It is an easy and fast way to navigate using the mouse, even if you are using Blender with a laptop with a trackpad.

1.2.1 Using the camera

In the navigation list, you will find an option that you can trigger with the Numpad 0 to set the view to the camera. Using the camera is extremely important in Blender because that is the only way you can save multiple views of a scene.

If you press the Numpad 0, you will see what the camera is framing (Figure 1.11).

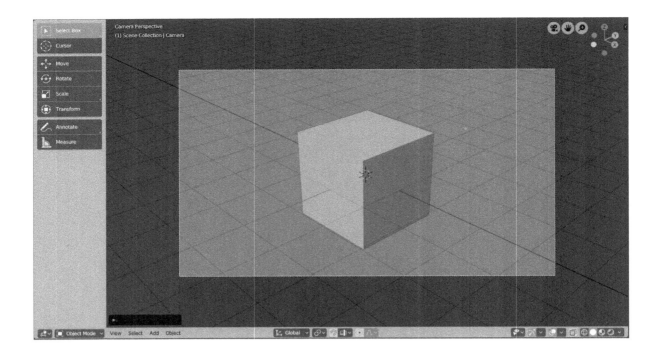

Figure 1.11 - *Camera view*

The camera is that object with a shape of a pyramid in your scene (Figure 1.12).

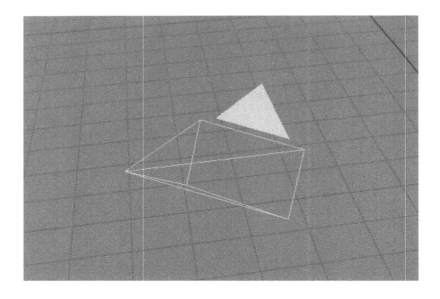

Figure 1.12 - *Camera Icon*

That is an object like any other in Blender that you can select and manipulate. You can move and rotate the camera to adjust the framing.

An important shortcut that was not on our list of 3D navigation options is the "Align Active Camera to View." It takes the active camera in the scene and aligns it to the same viewing angle you have at the moment.

You can trigger this option with the CTRL+ALT+Numpad 0 keys. That is an easy and fast way to align the camera. After that, you can still select the camera and use transformation shortcuts to adjust the framing.

Info: What is an Active Camera? Because we can have multiple cameras in a scene, Blender will set one of them as the Active. That is the camera used to display images in rendering. You can turn any camera as the active by selecting it and pressing the CTRL+Numpad 0 keys.

1.3 Object selection

The first time you open Blender after installing it on your computer, you will see a prompt asking you to pick the behavior of a few keys. In the quick setup, you will find an option called "Select With" that asks you about the selection. You can choose to select with the left or right mouse button.

In case you don't remember, you can always change these settings in the **Edit → Preferences...** menu and go to the Keymap tab. There you will see the preferences for how to select in Blender (Figure 1.13).

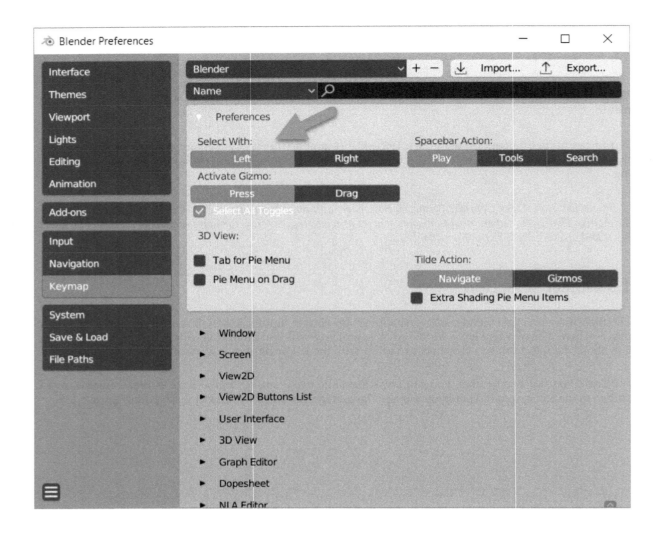

Figure 1.13 - *Selection preferences*

Since most graphical tools will work using the left mouse button for selection, you can choose this option to maintain the same pattern. You can also keep the old way Blender used before version 2.8 and choose the right button.

For the rest of this book, I will consider you are using the left button for selection.

Considering you are using the left mouse button for selection, you can click on any object in the Viewport to start a selection. The object will display an outline that will help you identify any selection (Figure 1.14).

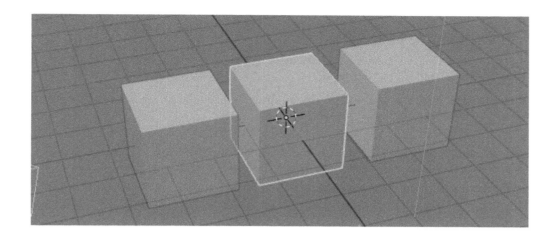

Figure 1.14 - *Outline for selected objects*

To add more objects to your selection, you can hold the SHIFT key and keep clicking on objects.

Info: When you select multiple objects in Blender, you will have something called Active Object. The Active Object will always be the last one you select.

Another way of handling selections is with the options at the Toolbar (Figure 1.15).

Figure 1.15 - *Selection options in Toolbar*

There you have three selection modes to choose:

- **Select box**: You will be able to draw a box on your screen to select all objects inside that area. The B key also triggers this selection mode.

- **Select circle**: Here, you will turn the mouse cursor into a circle where you will be able to paint the selection. The C key will trigger this mode.

- **Select lasso**: With the lasso, you will be able to draw an irregular shape with the mouse to select anything inside the area.

For architectural modeling, you will use a lot of the Select box and the B key.

Other useful shortcuts for selection also include:

- **A key**: Select all objects

- **ALT+A**: Remove all objects from the selection

- **CTRL+I**: Invert the selection

There are more options regarding selection that are available at the Select menu in the Viewport. All the selection shortcuts work on multiple editors in Blender.

1.4 Transformations and constraints

With an object selected, you can use options to transform them using three primary operations:

- Move

- Rotate

- Scale

You can trigger those transformations using either the buttons from the Toolbar or keyboard shortcuts. The buttons on the Toolbar will trigger a transformation widget that will help you apply the transformations visually (Figure 1.16).

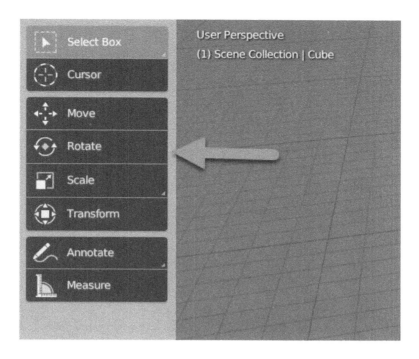

Figure 1.16 - *Toolbar buttons*

To use the widget, you have to pick the axis using the color code and click and drag with the mouse. The color codes are:

– **X-Axis**: Red

– **Y-Axis**: Green

– **Z-Axis**: Blue

And besides the buttons, you also have the keyboard shortcuts. Each transformation has the following shortcut:

– **G key**: Move

– **R key**: Rotate

– **S key**: Scale

Once you press each of those keys, you can easily constrain the transformation to an axis, using the corresponding key of that axis. For instance, if you press:

– **G key followed by the X key**: Move only on the X-Axis

– **R key followed by the Y key**: Rotate only on the Y-Axis

– **S key followed by the Z key**: Scale only on the Z-Axis

You can use any combination between transform keys and axis. For modeling purposes, you will find that using the shortcut is better for productivity and includes another benefit for architecture. You will be able to use precision transformations with numeric values.

That will be the main subject of Chapter 2, where we will discuss several options to work with precision modeling.

1.4.1 Duplicating objects

Now that you know how to select and transform objects, we can explore hoe to duplicate anything in Blender. If you have an object selected, you can press the SHIFT+D keys to duplicate the object.

After you trigger the duplicate option, a move transformation will start. You can press a key corresponding to the axis you wish to use for your copy, and constraint the location of your copy.

If you want to abort the object duplication, press the ESC key before you click to confirm the copy location. However, it will cancel the transformation only. You still have to press CTRL+Z to undo the duplication.

Tip: Another way of duplicating the object is with the Context Menu. With a right-click, you can open the menu and choose Duplicate Objects.

1.5 Shading modes in the Viewport

The Viewport of Blender is the place where you will see all the 3D models and work with the visual aspects of the project. For that reason, you should always try different shading modes to evaluate how your project is developing.

There are four shading modes available:

– Wireframe

– Solid

– Textured

– Rendered

You can change the shading model using either the Z key or the shading selector in your Viewport header (Figure 1.17).

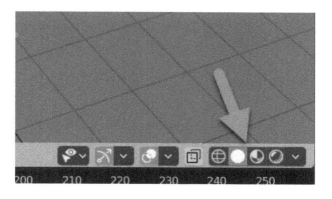

Figure 1.17 - *Shading mode*

On the left of your shading selector, you will also find a useful tool called X-Ray. When you activate that button, you will see and manage objects behind faces (Figure 1.18).

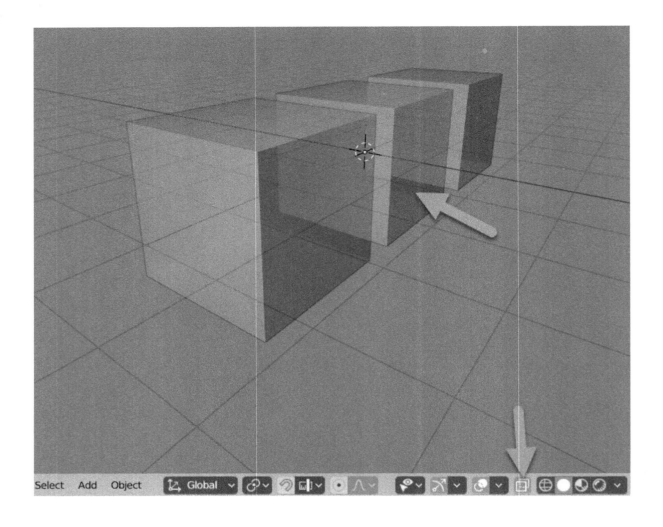

Figure 1.18 - X-Ray mode

That is important for selection purposes. For instance, when you have X-Ray enabled, you will be able to make a Box Selection with the mouse, and even objects behind faces will become selected by the tool.

1.6 Edit and Object Modes

A core fundamental in Blender is the use of work modes for objects you have selected. Regarding polygon modeling, you will usually swap between two main modes called Object and Edit. Until this point, you probably used only Object Mode to select and manipulate objects.

If you select one or multiple objects, you can change the work mode using the Viewport header. There you will find a selector that will give you all the options related to work modes for the selected objects (Figure 1.19).

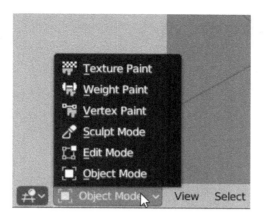

Figure 1.19 - *Work mode selector*

The other mode you should pay close attention is Edit Mode. Once you change to that mode, you will have access to the structure of your objects. In the case of polygon models, you will be able to select and transform:

- Vertices

- Edges

- Faces

You can choose what type of element you want to select and manipulate using the selector in the Viewport header (Figure 1.20).

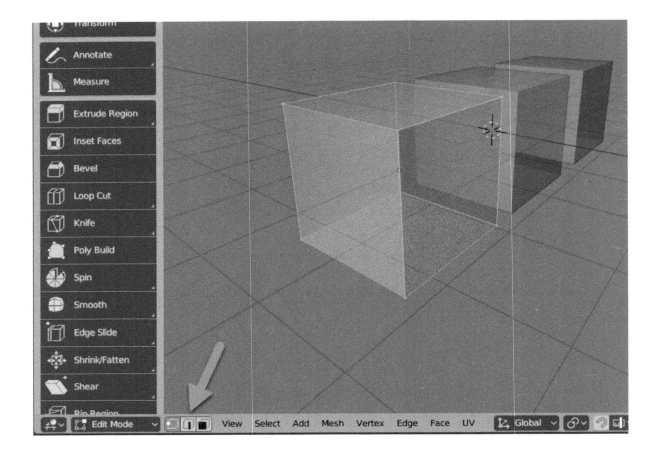

Figure 1.20 - *Element selection*

Since you have access to the structure of polygons using that mode, you can make all kinds of selections and changes to them. Selecting those parts and applying transformations like move, rotation, and scale will give you a lot of creative freedom.

For architectural modeling, you will usually swap between those two models, and Blender even has a keyboard shortcut to change from Object to Edit Modes quickly. You can press the Tab key to change from one to the other.

What should you do in each mode? To optimize your workflow:

– **Object Mode**: Apply transformations and select objects as a whole

– **Edit Mode**: Whenever you have to change the shape of an object or build a new shape from a 3D polygon primitive

It is entirely possible to apply transformations to objects in Edit Mode; however, you should take extra care when doing that operation. The main reason to be cautious is that those operations won't change the object origin point. You can manipulate and change polygons in Edit Mode, but the origin point will always stay at the same location.

Since that is the reference for object location, rotation, and scale operations in Object Mode, you could end up with a pivot point for the object far away from their main shape.

1.7 Creating objects and the 3D Cursor

How to create objects in Blender? In any part of the software, you will be able to create objects using the SHIFT+A keys. Regardless of editor or data, you are manipulating the shortcut will remain the same.

In your Viewport, you can press that same keys to open a menu will all options related to object creation (Figure 1.21). The same options are also available at the Add menu.

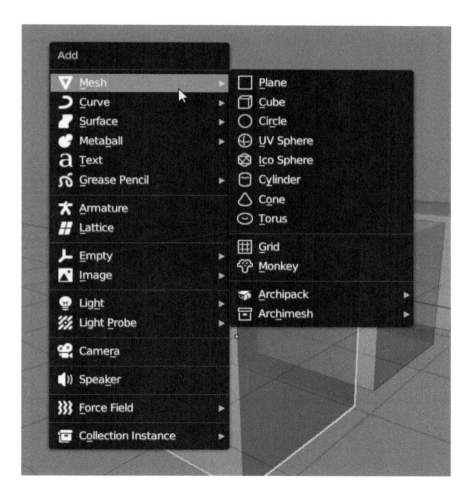

Figure 1.21 - *Object creation*

For architecture, you will usually create objects from the following groups:

– **Mesh**: Polygon objects used to start modeling like planes, cubes, and cylinders

– **Light**: Objects that can add light energy to the scene

– **Camera**: A particular type of object that can mark the viewing angle of a scene

Eventually, you will have to use other types of objects, but those are the main ones used for architecture.

1.7.1 3D Cursor and Snap

Where does Blender places new objects? Once you start to add new objects to the scene, you will notice that they will go to the same location of a small crosshair cursor in your Viewport. That is the 3D Cursor of Blender (Figure 1.22).

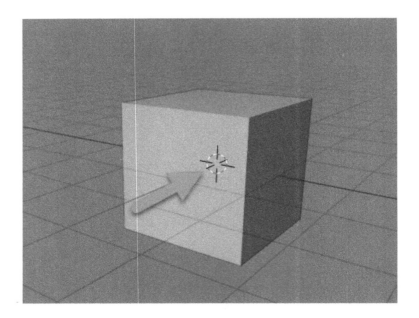

Figure 1.22 - 3D Cursor

The cursor has a lot of functions in Blender from marking the location of new objects to a temporary pivot point for transformations.

How to change the cursor location?

You can change the cursor location using several options:

– **With the mouse**: Hold the SHIFT key, and with a right-click, you can set the position of your cursor anywhere. You can also use the Cursor button in the Toolbar to click freely at the Viewport and relocate the cursor

– **With coordinates**: Press the N key in your Viewport to open the Properties tab. There you can open the View Tab and locate the 3D Cursor field. Change the coordinates there to move your cursor

– **With the snap tool**: You can also use the Snap to place the cursor next to other objects

The Snap tool in Blender is a powerful way to place the 3D Cursor in your scene using other object locations as the reference. For instance, if you look at Figure 1.23, you can see that our 3D Cursor is in a random position.

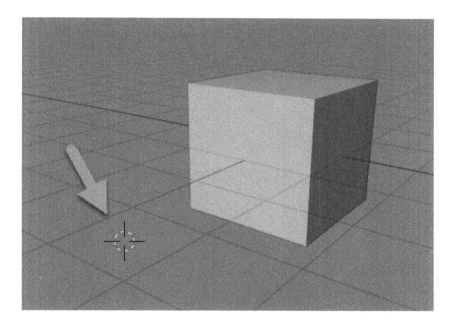

Figure 1.23 - *3D Cursor location*

To align the cursor to any object in your scene, you can select the object and press SHIFT+S. That will open the Snap options. From those options, you can pick the "Cursor to Selected." That option will make the cursor jump to the object location (Figure 1.24).

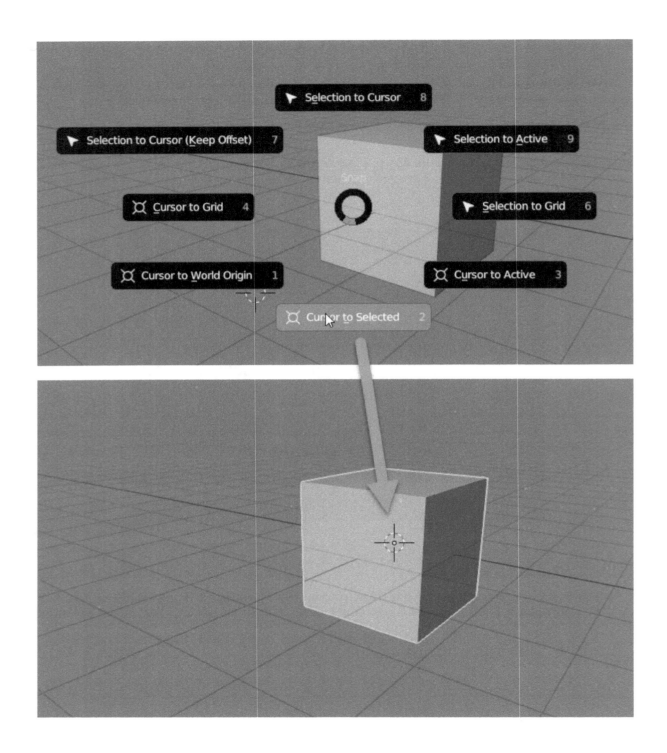

Figure 1.24 - Snap options

You can even align the cursor based on elements of a polygon model. For instance, we can go to Edit Mode and select a vertex of an object. Press the SHIFT+S key and choose the "Cursor to Selected" again to align the cursor (Figure 1.25).

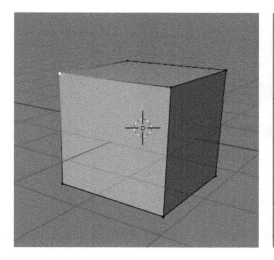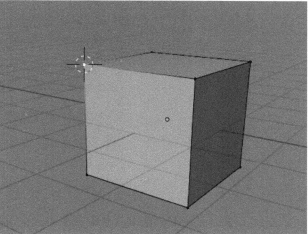

Figure 1.25 - *Cursor with Edit Mode*

One of the benefits of aligning the cursor in Edit Mode is the possibility of controlling object origin.

1.7.2 Changing object origin point

Once the cursor is at the location you wish to use as the new origin point you can use the **Object → Set Origin → Origin to 3D Cursor** menu. By choosing this option, you will be able to change the location of any origin point to the cursor location.

That is a powerful way of controlling the reference point for 3D models in architecture like furniture and external references.

Tip: The same options are also available in the context menu. You can right-click with an object selected and open the context menu to find both the Set Origin and Snap.

1.7.3 Pivot point

Some operations in Blender like a rotation will use the origin point of objects as the pivot point. In some case, you may want to use another location as the pivot point. The 3D Cursor can also work as a pivot point if you change the settings of a particular panel in Blender.

The Viewport header has a menu called Pivot Point, where you can choose how Blender will handle those points (Figure 1.26).

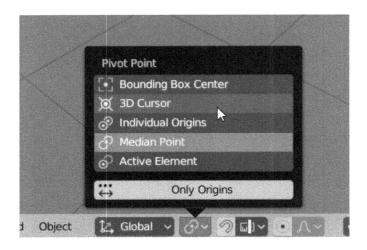

Figure 1.26 - Pivot point

By default, a pivot point will always be the central location for a selection. If you change the settings to use the 3D Cursor, you will have full control over your pivot point.

That will work for all transformations and not only to the rotation.

1.8 Saving files and projects

After a period working on a project in Blender, you will probably want to save your progress to continue later or to make a backup of your work. To save a project in Blender, you will have to use the **File → Save As...** menu.

You will pick a location for the file and give it a name. That will write a file with an extension of ".blend" in your hard drive. As you progress with the project, Blender may create additional files with an extension of ".blend1" that is a backup of your main project.

Good practice in architectural projects is to save your progress with different file names, which will make it easy for you to rollback to a previous state of the scene.

In Blender, you will even find a tool that will help you add a numeric suffix to the file (Figure 1.27).

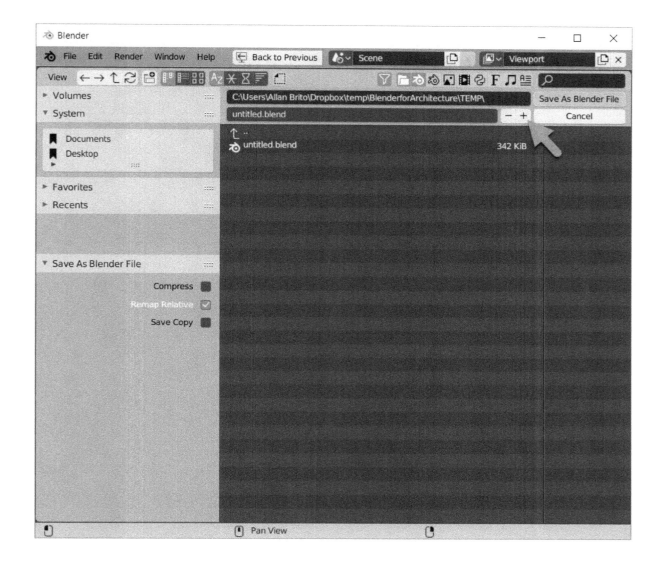

Figure 1.27 - *Numeric increment*

By using a numeric increment to your file name, you will be able to set a name for a project like "floor-planviews.blend" and with the "+" button you will get "floorplanviews1.blend" as a result.

Besides getting the file names in the order, you should also pick a different folder for each project. Because Blender might keep a few files, you are producing on that folder if you open the **Edit → Preferences...** menu and go to the File Paths tab (Figure 1.28).

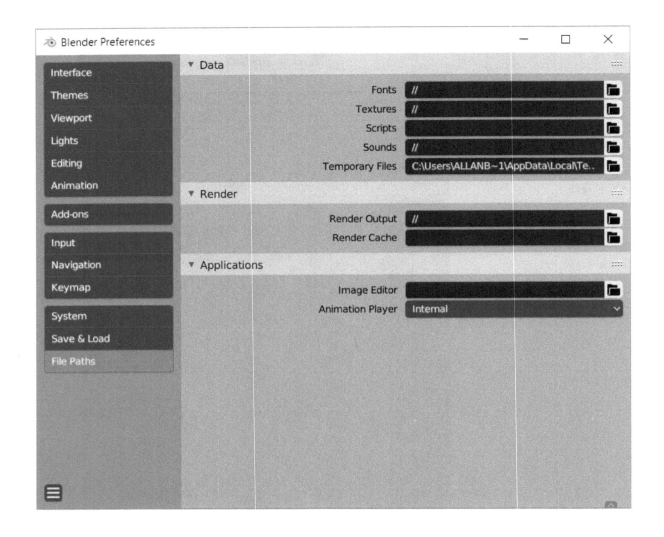

Figure 1.28 - File Paths

You will notice that some paths will have a "// "as the location. That means it is using the current file location instead of a fixed folder in your computer. That means Blender will store textures and the render results in the same folder you have the project file saved.

What is next?

You now have a great understanding of the Blender 2.8 user interface and primary tools to manipulate and create 3D objects. The next natural step for us is to move forward and learn how to do precision modeling.

You will find that Blender has a robust set of tools regarding numeric transformations, which will allow you to have precise control on how you create 3D Objects.

The next two chapters will cover a lot of aspects regarding 3D modeling for architecture, from using numeric transformations to the modeling of architectural elements like walls, windows, and doors.

Chapter 2 - Precision modeling for architecture

The first step in a visualization project is the modeling stage, where you have to get your ideas and transform them into 3D Models. From those 3D models, you will apply materials, textures, and lights to create the visualization for architecture.

For architecture, you will have to use precise transformations and numeric values to define the shape of your 3D model, and Blender can help a lot in that stage.

The following chapter will explain how to use the precision modeling options of Blender that will help you work faster and make better architectural models.

Here is a summary of what you will learn:

- Use numeric input for modeling

- Choose between Metric and Imperial units

- Add units to any numeric input for modeling

- Make use of local coordinates for modeling

- Create walls using the extrude tool

- Use the Spin tool to create round shapes

- Editing 3D models to stretch and change their forms

2.1 Precise transformations (Numeric)

One of the critical aspects of working with architectural modeling is the ability to use numeric transformations. Unlike many projects that deal with only visual references and proportions, in architecture, we have to make sure all lengths and measurements have the correct values.

In Blender, we have an easy way to work with precise transformations. All you have to do is type the value you need in the keyboard while in a transformation. For instance, if you have to move an object five units, you can type five and press Return to confirm.

Here is how it works:

1. Select an object

2. Trigger a move transformation with the G key

3. Pick an axis for the transformation. Press the X key for the X-axis

4. Type 5 in your keyboard

5. Press Return to confirm your transformation

It is incredibly easy to make numeric transformations using this method. You can also use negative values to move your object in the opposite direction.

Here are the values you can use for each type of transformation:

- **Move**: Use values based on the unit system you have in use. For instance, you can use a value of one or minus one to move an object. You must pick an axis to transform with precision.

- **Rotation**: You can use degrees to rotate objects. The value can be positive or negative to rotate objects in the opposite direction. Like the move transformation, you also must choose an axis to apply any transformation.

- **Scale**: Here, we have something different, because scale transformations use a proportion value with the number one being 100% of the object size. For instance, if you want to increase the object size by 20%, you should use 1.2 as the value. You don't have to pick an axis if you're going to apply the scale as a whole. But, you can choose an axis to stretch or shrink an object in one direction only.

Whenever you have an ongoing transformation in Blender, you can cancel it anytime by pressing the ESC key.

If you want to have a visual reference for the values you are typing for transformations, you can use the status area of the Viewport. When you type a value for a transformation, it will appear on the lower-left corner of your screen (Figure 2.1).

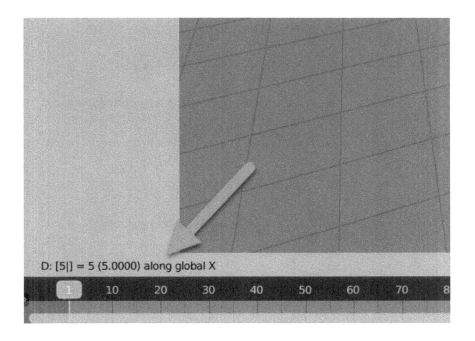

Figure 2.1 - *Numeric transformations*

Besides having the ability to use numeric transformations for modeling by typing values in your keyboard, Blender also has a special mode called "Advanced Mode" where you can make expressions.

To trigger advance mode, you have to press the = key before typing any value for a transformation. When you are in advanced mode, Blender will display brackets in the status area of your Viewport.

What can you do with advanced mode? You can type expressions like:

```
(3+8)x20
```

After typing the expression, you can press the Return key for Blender to evaluate the results and apply the transformation (Figure 2.2).

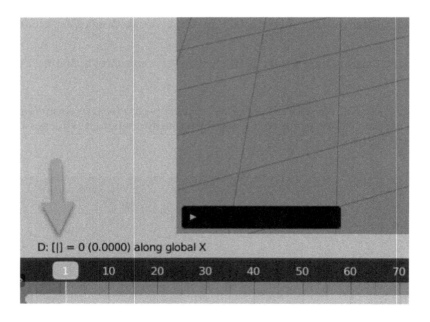

Figure 2.2 - *Advanced mode*

That is a powerful way to have better control over 3D modeling for architecture, and you can perform quick math operations directly in Blender.

2.2 Using the metric or imperial system for modeling

What type of units Blender uses for all modeling operations? If you don't explicitly choose a unit system for your modeling operations, Blender will use something called BU or Blender Units.

It is an abstract unit that resembles what we have for meters in the real-world. However, you can also choose among the Metric or Imperial system for units. Go to the Scene tab in the Properties editor, and you will find the Units options (Figure 2.3).

Figure 2.3 - Units options

There you can choose between the Metric or Imperial system.

2.2.1 Using the Metric System

If you decide to use the Metric system for your modeling operations, you will immediately see a few changes in Blender. The first change is that all measurements now have a suffix with the unit. It can be either "m" for meters or "cm" for centimeters (Figure 2.4).

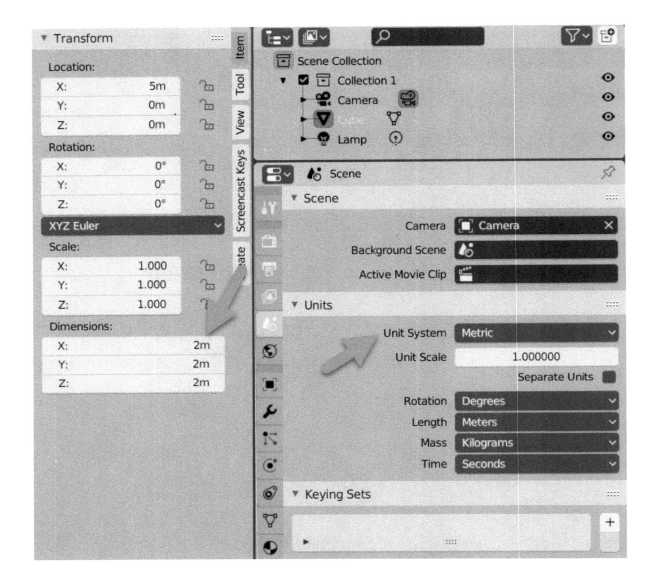

Figure 2.4 - Units using the Metric System

Notice from Figure 2.4 that you have a specific unit for lengths. That is not just a visual reference, and you can also use the suffix for modeling. For instance, you will be able to type:

- 2m

- 4cm

- 0.5m

- 30mm

All those values will generate the correct transformation for modeling, which is crucial for architectural modeling. If you enter the advanced mode, you can also mix units and make expressions such as:

- 4m+50cm

- 300mm+9m

- 50cm+1.5m

The use of a unity system will help you maintaining control over large modeling projects in Blender.

2.2.2 Using the Imperial System

For artists and professionals living in countries where you must work with the Imperial system for modeling, you also have all the necessary options to work with precision in Blender. When you pick the Imperial System for modeling, you will start to see all values for lengths in feet.

In architectural modeling, it is common to use a mix of two units to display lengths. Unlike the Metric system where you can use fractions to represent a measurement of 1.5 meters in the Imperial system, you will mix feet and inches.

To use mixed units for lengths in Blender, you must enable the "Separate Units" right below the unit system selector. Once you activate the option, you will see lengths displaying with two units (Figure 2.5).

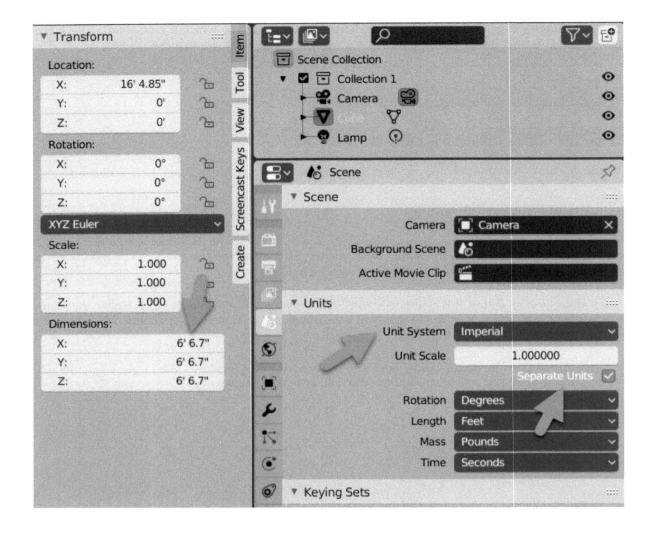

Figure 2.5 - Imperial units

After choosing the Imperial system and setting the "Separate Units" option, you will see values in your interface to reflect that change.

You will be able to type:

– 6ft

– 6'

– 2in

– 3"

All those values will give you lengths in the Imperial system. To mix units and have full control over your modeling, you must use advanced mode for transformations. Before typing any length, press the = key and start typing mixed values:

- 5ft2in

- 3/4in

- 4'3"

- 2'8/9"

All those notations will work and give you exact lengths for the Imperial system.

2.2.3 Displaying lengths and fixing scales

During the modeling stage of a project, you might want to check if a particular length is correct or have a visual reference of measurement. We have a few options to display distances in Blender.

The first one is the ability to show lengths for any selected edge in Edit Mode. To enable that option, you must go to Edit Mode and look for the Overlays options. There you will find in the "Measurement" options the "Edge Length" (Figure 2.6).

Figure 2.6 - *Edge Length*

If you enable this option, you will see the measurement for any selected edge in Edit Mode (Figure 2.7).

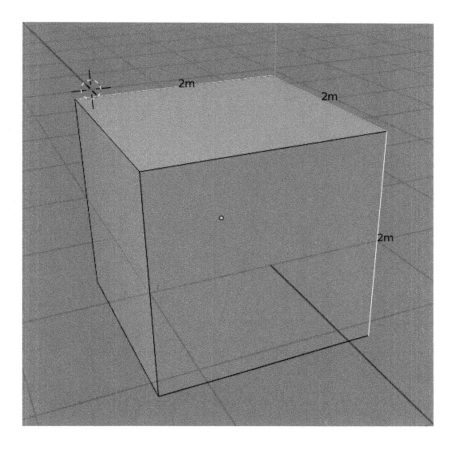

Figure 2.7 - *Lengths for edges*

That will work great for quick evaluations in Edit Mode, but once you go back to Object Mode, the values will disappear.

Another option that will give you a more persistent way of displaying lengths is the "Measure" option in the Toolbar. If you turn on the tool, you will be able to draw a ruler on your Viewport by clicking and dragging (Figure 2.8).

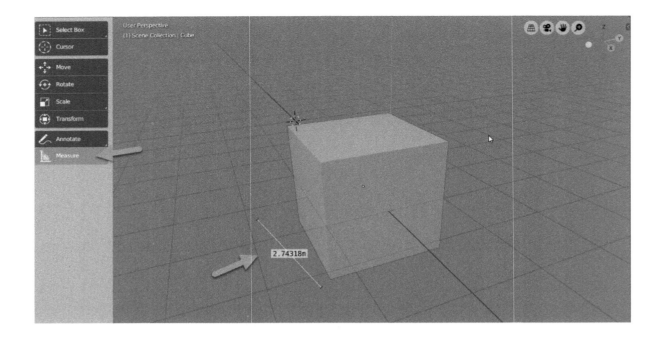

Figure 2.8 - Ruler with measurement

Having a ruler is a great help to evaluate distances, but what about precision? You can make Blender snap the ruler to specific points by pressing the ^ key in your keyboard. The precision option will appear when you place the mouse above the start or endpoints of your ruler. Your cursor will show an icon like a four-point "star."

Press and hold the ^ key or the SHIFT key and move the ruler above an edge. It will snap to a face and show the length for that object (Figure 2.9).

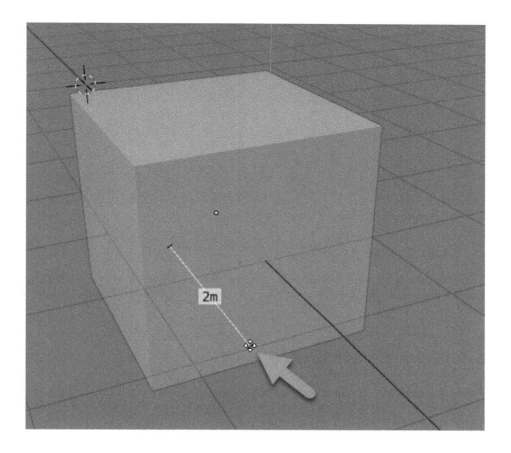

Figure 2.9 - *Ruler with snap*

To remove any ruler from your Viewport, you can select it using the start or endpoints and press the Del key. Do not try to select or move the ruler using the middle line. It will "break" the line and show an angle instead.

What should you do if your lengths in Blender are not accurate with the object?

There is a situation where you might have to apply a fix to the scales to display them correctly. That will occur after a scale transformation. For instance, if you have an edge that shows a length of 2 units and apply a scale of 0.5 to reduce the size by 50%, it should display a distance of 1 unit.

If you follow the procedure, the results won't show 1 unit, but two instead. That is not an error from Blender, but a way to show values based on scales. Whenever you apply a scale operation to a 3D object, it will keep the original size and display a version of it using the proportion you set during a scale.

That means, after a scale transformation, you won't have an object with the size you intended during the transform. You can easily verify that in the properties tab at the Viewport. If an object has a scale factor different than 1, it means it does not display real measurements (Figure 2.10).

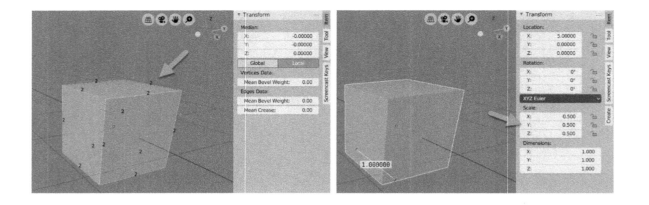

Figure 2.10 - *Properties tab scale*

How to fix that? Simple, apply the scale transformation with a CTRL+A key or use the **Object** → **Apply** → **Scale** menu. That will turn any scale factor back to one and make Blender display lengths based on object size.

2.3 Local and global coordinates

In CAD tools, you will find that by using coordinate systems, you will find the concept of global and relative coordinates that will help drawing and modeling. For Blender, you will find another essential concept called local and global coordinates.

The global coordinate system is what you will find in almost all 3D software with six-axis using positive and negative values for X, Y, and Z. They will never change.

What are local coordinates? The system works exactly like the global coordinates with the difference of being attached to an object. Since it has a direct relation to an object, it will receive the same transformations.

For instance, if you have a plane that is representing an architectural element like a ramp. With the global coordinate system, all the plane axis will have the same orientation. However, by applying a rotation of 45 degrees in the Y-axis, you will make the local coordinates for that particular object also rotate (Figure 2.11).

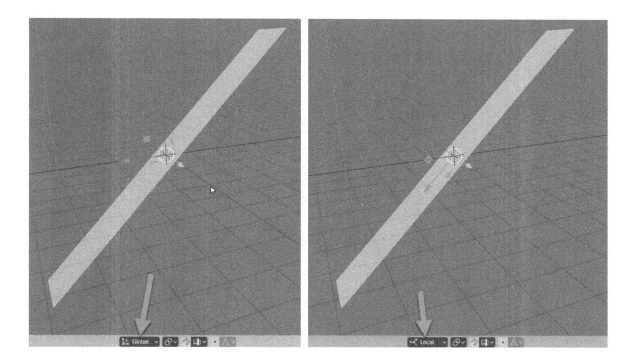

Figure 2.11 - *Local coordinates for plane*

Each object has a unique local coordinate system, and they can become useful for modeling.

How to use such a coordinate system?

In Blender, you can press the key corresponding to the axis in which you want to constraint a transformation. That will use the global system. If you press the axis key twice, it will use the local system.

For instance, if you try to move the plane in the Z-axis after that 45 degrees rotation, you will see a different result using the global or local coordinates. The local coordinates will move parallel to the plane, while the global system will use the vertical axis (Figure 2.12).

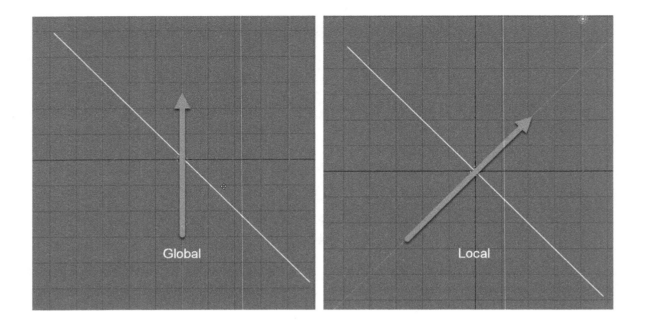

Figure 2.12 - *Global and local transformations*

Remember that your local coordinate system receives all transformations for each object. If you have to apply or make a transformation aligned to the object, use that to speed up modeling and make a few models a lot easier to build.

Tip: If you want to keep the local coordinate system aligned after a rotation, do not apply the rotation transformation with the CTRL+A key. If you do that it will reset the axis and make it aligned to the global system.

2.4 Precise modeling with extrudes

One of the most used tools for 3D modeling in architecture is the extrude tool not only in Blender but any software that has a base in polygon modeling. By applying the same precision techniques discussed at the beginning of this chapter, we can make extrusions with an excellent level of numeric control.

How to start an extrude? Simple, you can select one or multiple objects and go to Edit Mode. There you can the extrude button in the Toolbar or the E key. For precision control, it will be much better to use the E key shortcut.

The reason is simple; it won't involve the mouse. If you decide to go with the button, you will start the extrude with the cursor. That won't give you the immediate option to provide a numeric value.

For instance, you can take an object like the one shown in Figure 2.13 and select one edge. If that should represent a wall with a height of 3.2 meters or 10'5.98".

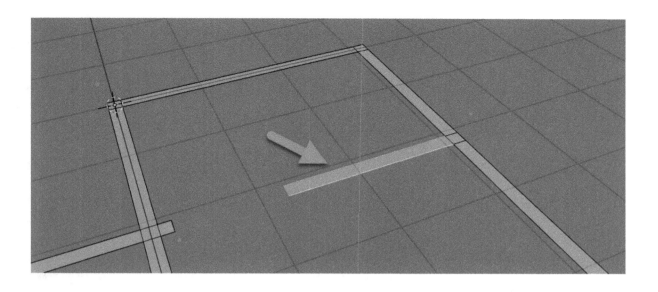

Figure 2.13 - *Selected edge*

We could apply an extrude with the following procedure:

1. Press the E key

2. Press the Z key to constraint the extrude to the Z-axis

3. Type 3.2

4. Press Return to confirm

If you want to use the Imperial System:

1. Press the E key

2. Press the Z key to constraint the extrude to the Z-axis

3. Press the = key

4. Type 10'5.98" or 10.49'

5. Press Return to confirm

For the Imperial System, I will assume you are using the "Separate Units" option.

That will result in the following extrude shown in Figure 2.14.

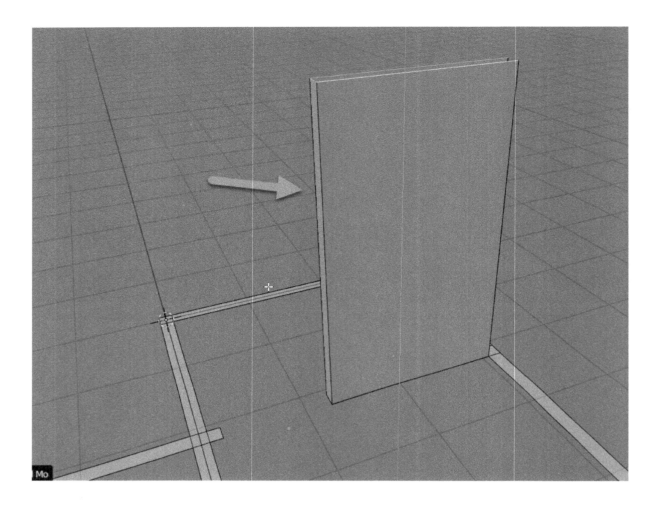

Figure 2.14 - *Extrude results*

Regarding the extrude tool, you will always have to use the corresponding axis key to align your results. Unless you have a face selected, which will apply the extrude in a parallel direction.

Tip: You can always cancel an extrude if you make a mistake using the ESC key. Just remember that using the ESC key will cancel the extrude, but not the transformation. If you want to cancel the extrude you must also press the CTRL+Z keys to undo the full operation.

2.5 Making walls with precise dimensions

You can use the same extrude tool allied with precise transformations to start modeling walls on any project in Blender. For instance, if we have a floorplan like the one shown in Figure 2.15 and that you have to reproduce in Blender.

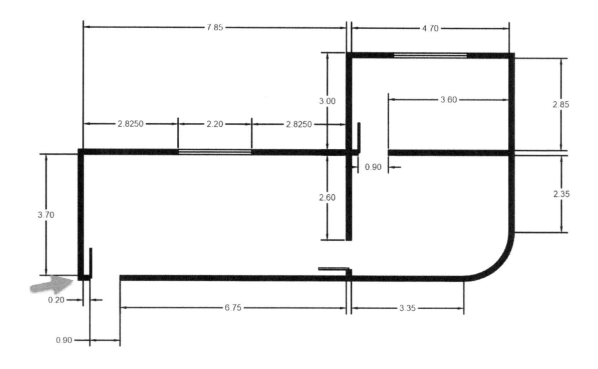

Figure 2.15 - *Floorplan*

We can start with a small plane representing one of the edges for that wall. At Figure 2.15, we have a corner of the wall marked with an arrow. That will be our starting point.

Assuming the walls have 15cm in thickness, we can start creating the objects necessary to make the full model.

Info: We will use the Metric System for the example, but you can easily use the Imperial System replacing the measurements. Just remember to enable the "Separate Units" option.

Add a plane to the scene with the SHIFT+A keys, and since this object has a default size of 2 meters by 2 meters, we need to scale it down. The scale factor we need is 0.075 because 0.15/2 = 0.075.

Press the S key and type "0.075" and press Return to confirm. Don't forget to press the CTRL+A key to apply the scale. Turn on the "Edge Length" from the Overlays menu to make sure it has the correct size (Figure 2.16).

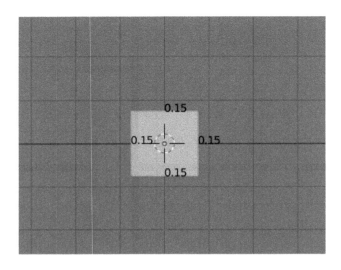

Figure 2.16 - Plane with the correct size

In Edit Mode, select the edge of your plane and apply the first extrude. Since we are using edges, you will have to constraint the extrude to the Y-axis. Press the E key and after that the Y key. Type the length of your wall, as shown in Figure 2.15, which is 3.5 and press Return. The result will be your first wall (Figure 2.17).

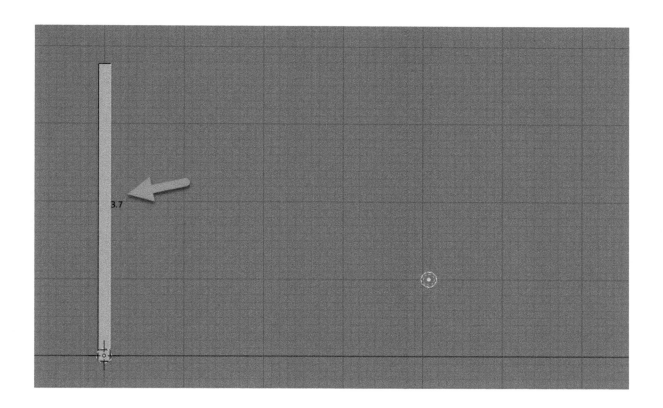

3.7

Figure 2.17 - First wall

If you follow all the measurements from the floorplan and repeat the process, you will end up with all the walls. At this moment, you can skip the round corner. We will make a rounded corner in section 2.6 in this chapter.

Notice that for windows we will make a segment using the extrude. For the door space, you will leave that with no faces. Leave the gap between the edges empty (Figure 2.18).

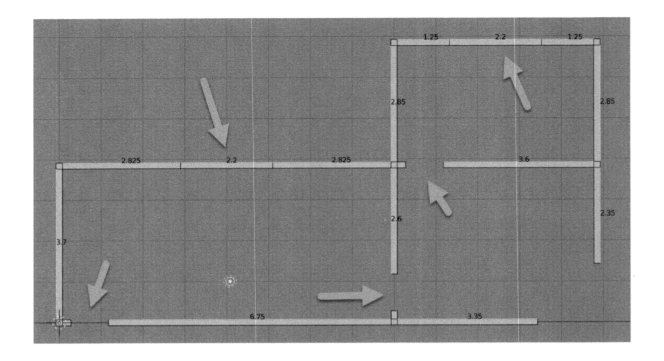

Figure 2.18 - *Windows and doors*

To leave that gap empty, you can apply the extrude and erase the face at the end, or you can also not use the extrude and instead duplicate the edge using the SHIFT+D keys.

When you have all the walls in place, we can select all objects from the model with the A key and apply another extrude. Since it is now an extrude based on faces, you don't have to constraint that to an axis.

The room has a window, and you can easily prepare to use such an object with a segmented extrude. Instead of going with a single extrude for the wall height, we will use three.

Why three? The first one will be for the window sill with a height of 1.2. After you apply the first extrude, you should remove from the selection of any faces marking window spaces. In this case, you can remove the face marked by Figure 2.19.

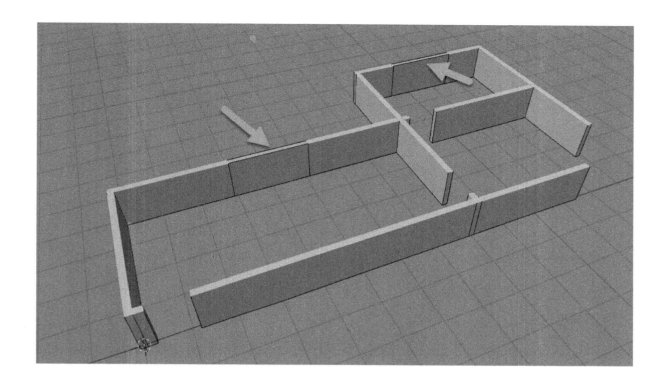

Figure 2.19 - *Face removed from selection*

To remove a face from selection, you can hold the SHIFT key and left-click on it twice.

After you remove the face from the selection, you can apply the next two extrudes of 1.1 and 1.3. In the end, you will have the full wall height of 3.6 (Figure 2.20).

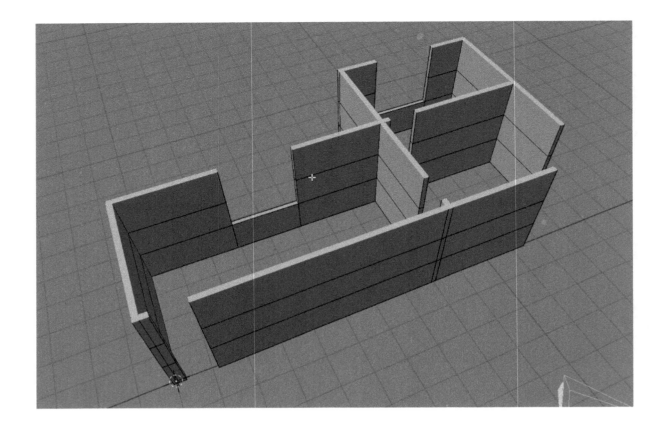

Figure 2.20 - Wall height after extrudes

We have some missing parts in the model, like the curved corner and loose pieces at the top of our window and door. We will finish the rest of this model until the chapter end.

2.6 Round shapes and corners for walls

Having a round corner in a model like the one we have currently modeling could represent a challenge if you don't have the correct tools available. Luckily, Blender has something perfect to create round corners for walls. With the Spin tool, we can make that type of shape.

Before we use the Spin tool, which is available at the Toolbar on the left, we must follow a few rules to get our rounded wall:

- The pivot point will be the 3D Cursor location
- Any geometry created by the Spin will be perpendicular to the view you have of the scene at the moment

To comply with those two rules, we must:

1. Place the 3D Cursor in the center point of your rounded wall projection

2. Set the view to the top

First, we can place the 3D Cursor location. Since the wall radius is equal to 1.5 meters, we can make a temporary edge starting from the vertex shown in Figure 2.21.

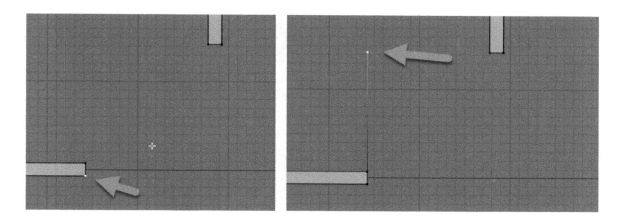

Figure 2.21 - Vertex location and extrude

Still, in Figure 2.21, you can see the extrude with 1.5 in the Y-axis. Keep the vertex marked in the right side of Figure 2.21 selected and press SHIFT+S. That will call the snap option and choose "Cursor to Selected," and your 3D Cursor should go to the same location as that vertex.

Info: You can erase the temporary edge later.

That is the center point of our Spin. How does Spin work? Select the edge where you want to start making the round wall (Figure 2.22).

Figure 2.22 - Starting edge

Press the 7 key in your Numpad, and you will be all set to start a Spin.

Once you press the icon for the Spin, you will see a blue arc on top of your selected edge. Click and drag that arc in the direction you wish to create the rounded wall. When you release the mouse, use the small menu that will appear to choose the exact Angle for the Spin as -90 degrees (Figure 2.23).

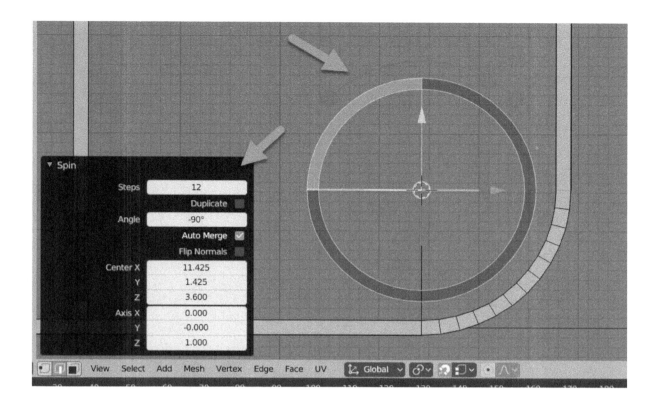

Figure 2.23 - *Spin Angle*

The Steps option will segment the arc and give you more polygons to represent the shape. A value of 12 for this example will generally be enough.

After the Spin we apply the extrude to the rounded wall, by selecting all faces of the wall and pressing the E key. You can make three extrudes to match the segments for the wall (Figure 2.24).

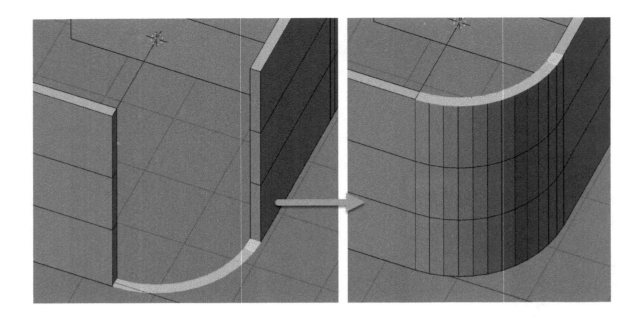

Figure 2.24 - Wall with extrude

As a last step for the Spin, we can make sure all vertices from the resulting object have had a connection. Press the A key to select all vertices and with a right-click call the context menu. Choose **Merge Vertices → By Distance**. It will remove all duplicated vertices if you keep the distance to zero.

2.7 Connecting loose parts of 3D models

At the top of our model, you will see some parts that still need some work, especially regarding connections. The top of windows and doors remain separated. How to connect them?

For that particular task, we can use a tool in Blender called Bridge Faces. To use such a tool, we have to select two faces, like the ones shown in Figure 2.25, representing the top of our door. It is essential to be parallel faces.

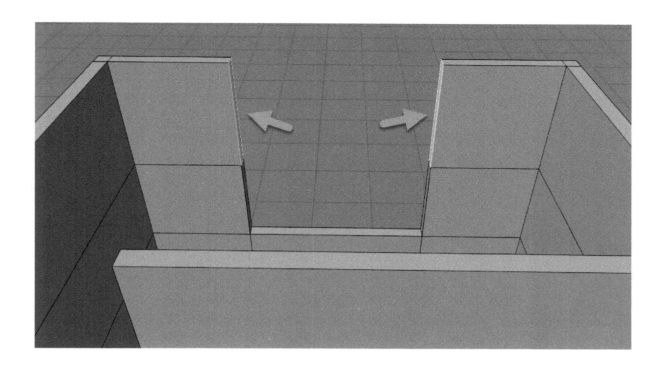

Figure 2.25 - Selected faces

With the faces selected, you can right-click to call the context menu for faces, and there you will see the Bridge Faces option. Pick that option, and you will connect the top faces.

Repeat the same process with the faces of your window, and you will connect the upper parts of the wall (Figure 2.26).

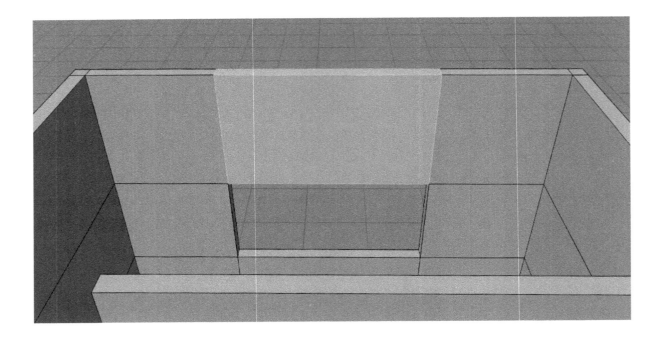

Figure 2.26 - *Connected faces*

Unfortunately, you must select two faces at the time to use this option.

2.8 Stretching and resizing architectural models

What if you got a distance with the wrong length? Is it possible to resize a 3D model in Blender? Sure, you can resize any model in Blender using Edit Mode.

The process is simple and requires you only to select the parts you wish to resize. For instance, we have to get the same model and extend the walls by 2 meters (Figure 2.27).

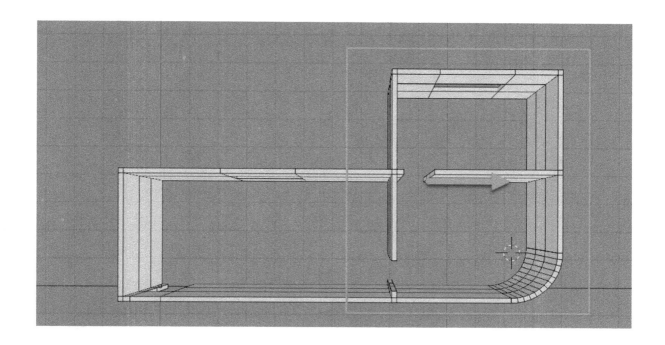

Figure 2.27 - *Walls to extend*

Select the 3D model you want to change and go to Edit Mode. In this case, you want to perform that action in Edit Mode. There you will use the vertex selection model to make a selection that will have only the parts you need to move.

The easiest option for that selection will be the B key for a Box selection (Figure 2.28).

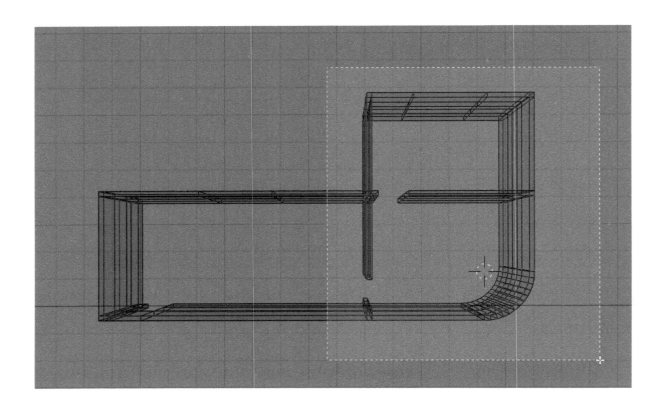

Figure 2.28 - *Box selection*

Change your shading mode to Wireframe to get all vertices. You can do that with the Z key.

Once you have the vertices selected, press the G key and the X key. That will constrain the transformation to the X-axis. Type 2, and you will expand the walls with no need to change your 3D model (Figure 2.29).

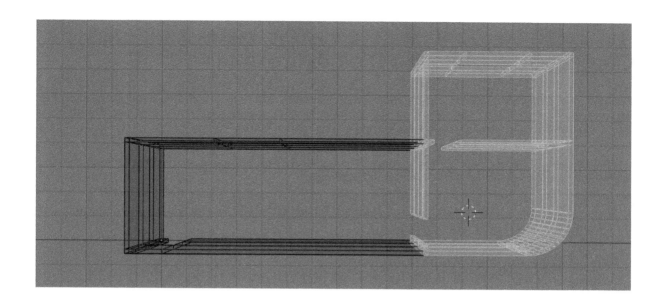

Figure 2.29 - *Resized walls*

If you need to resize walls in Blender, always select the shape you have to edit and use the G key with a numeric value. Seep in mind that you have to be extra careful to use such operation with a 3D model that has textures applied because it could deform the material.

What is next?

Now that you know how to work with precision modeling for architecture in Blender, we can move forward in the modeling subject to expand even more our skill set.

The next step is to use tools like modifiers to build a lot more complex models.

Chapter 3 - Architectural modeling tools

In architectural modeling, you will need a few additional skills and tools to build and edit 3D models. For instance, have you noticed how many buildings have symmetrical shapes? They also use a pattern to make construction and design easier, which could also help in 3D modeling.

The following chapter will give you some of those skills as a complement of the previous chapter, where you learned how to work with precision modeling.

Here you will learn how to cut and separate models and also use tools like Add-ons to make architectural elements like windows and doors quickly.

Here is a list of what you will learn in this chapter:

- Manage and edit architectural models by cutting and separating them
- Create 3D models based on symmetry
- Use repeating patterns to create large surfaces
- Manage and use Add-ons for modeling
- Create doors and windows for architectural models

3.1 Cutting and slicing architectural models

After you make a full architectural model, you may realize that you might have to cut or separate that model to either make derivate objects or exclude parts of your main shape. You can cut and make segments to 3D models in Blender using a tool called Loop Cut.

You will find the Loop Cut icon at the Toolbar with the option to also use a keyboard shortcut. The shortcut is CTRL+R, and it will give you a much faster way to cut objects in Blender.

To access and use the Loop Cut, you will have to first go to Edit Mode with a selected object. Once in Edit Mode, you can trigger the tool using the CTRL+R keys, and you will start the cut.

What do you need to cut any 3D Model using a Loop Cut? After triggering the tool, you will have to make two choices:

- The direction of your cut
- Placement of the cut

The first step is to choose a direction with the mouse cursor. When you trigger the Loop Cut, you will have to place the mouse over an edge, and your cut will be perpendicular to that edge (Figure 3.1).

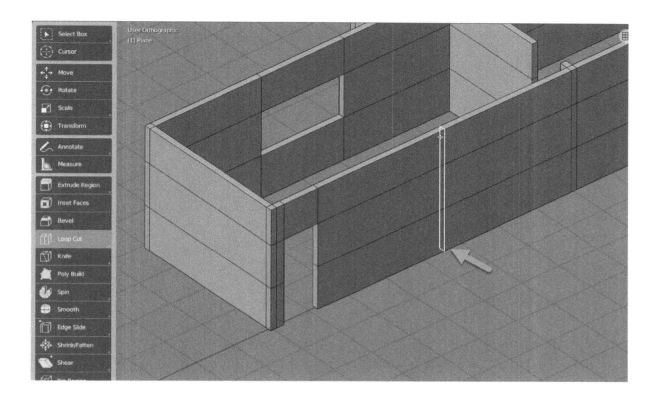

Figure 3.1 - *Loop Cut direction*

At this moment, you can also choose how many cuts you wish to make. Using the mouse wheel, you can add or remove cuts. The option is available if you use the plus and minus keys of your keyboard (Figure 3.2).

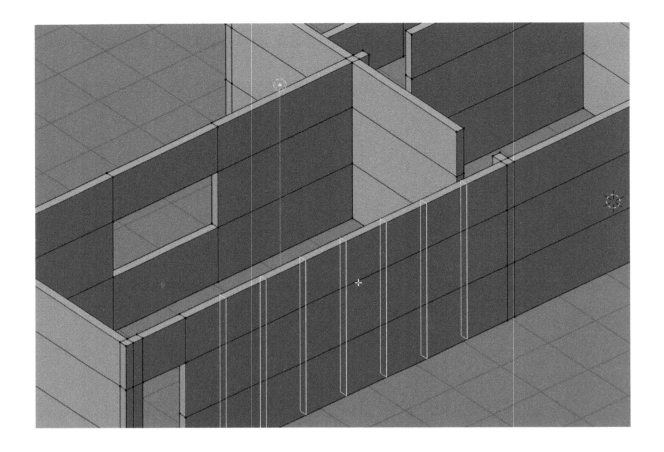

Figure 3.2 - *Number of cuts*

Regardless of how many cuts you choose, you must decide where to place the new cuts. You will left-click once to confirm the direction of your cut and then move the cursor to pick a location for the cuts. Use a left-click again to confirm the location.

What if you want the cuts at the middle? In this case, you can skip the last click and press the ESC key. It will keep the cuts in the middle and cancel the placement of your new edges.

A few things to consider for your cuts in architectural models:

– The tool will try to make a loop in your model adding edges

– Only edges with four sides can receive a cut

– Any face that has fewer or more than four edges will interrupt the loop

– Even with new edges, your model will remain a single object

3.1.1 Separating models

How to separate objects for modeling? You may want to split a 3D Model into two objects or more for numerous reasons, and with the Separate tool in Blender, you can do that easily.

The only requirement to separate objects is to select the parts you wish to split. For instance, at Figure 3.3, we will choose only part of a 3D Model that we will separate.

You can activate the Separate option using the P key in Edit Mode or the **Mesh** → **Separate** menu.

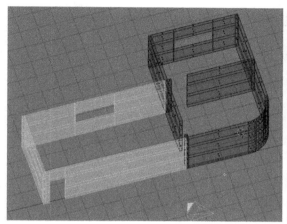 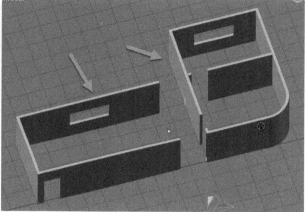

Figure 3.3 - *Selected parts*

At the Separate options you will have to choose from:

- **Selected**: Makes a new object based on what you have selected
- **By Material**: Makes a new object based on individual materials
- **By Loose Parts**: Makes a new object from unconnected parts of your model

Choose the Selected option, and you will have a new object from your selection.

3.2 Mirroring models based on symmetry

In architecture models, you will eventually see symmetry in a lot of projects for both aesthetics and economic reasons. Having a building with two symmetrical sides will be easier to design and build.

We have a tool in Blender that can help to make 3D Models based on a mirrored version of a shape. The Mirror modifier can take any part of a 3D object and created an inverted copy of the model.

For instance, if you look at the model shown in Figure 3.4, you will see that it has a perfect symmetry. The walls on the left are a perfect mirror image from the walls on the right.

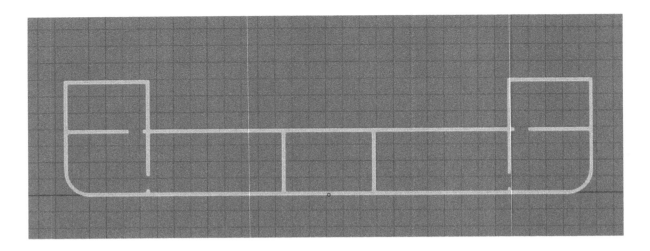

Figure 3.4 - Mirrored model

To apply a Mirror modifier to any object, you will have to first locate the option in the Modifiers tab at the Properties editor. There you will see an option "Add Modifier." Open the modifier list and choose the Mirror option (Figure 3.5).

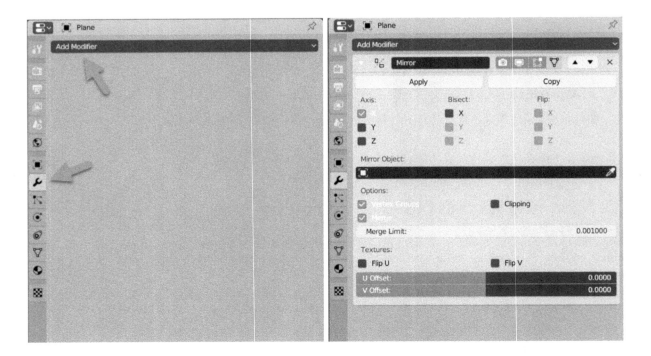

Figure 3.5 - *Mirror modifier*

Before we go to the settings for the Mirror modifier, you should make a small adjustment to the model based on the way you need the mirrored copy. The adjustment has a direct relation to the axis used to make the mirror object.

How Blender chooses the pivot point for the axis? It will use the 3D object origin point as the pivot point for the Mirror. The origin point is the small orange dot the will also serve as a reference for object co-ordinate location.

The mirrored copy will have the same reference location to the origin point as the source 3D model. For instance, if you place the origin point of your model at the edge and apply the mirror. The copy will also have the same location as the origin.

In Figure 3.6, you can see the difference from a mirror copy using an origin point at the source object and other far away.

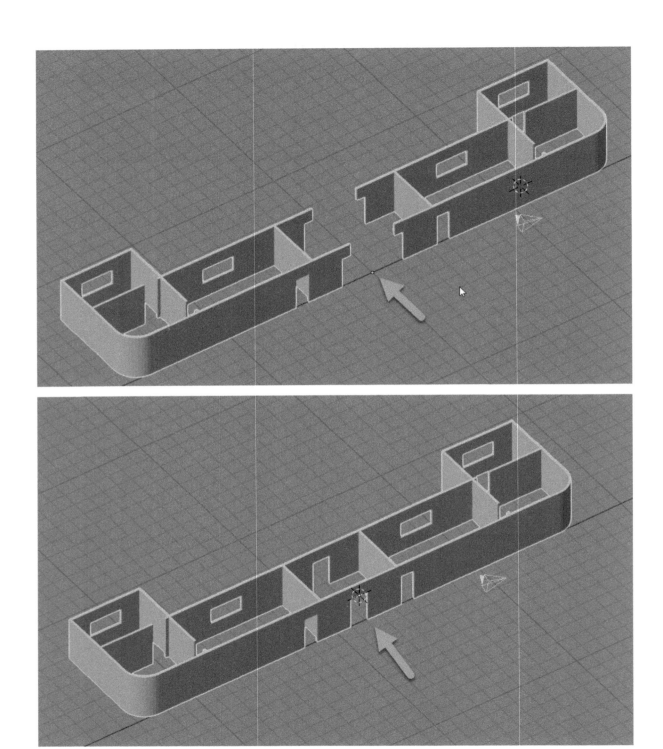

Figure 3.6 - *Origin point comparison*

How to move your origin point? If you want to move your origin point for any object, we will have to use the 3D Cursor. First, go to Edit Mode and select a vertex or edge where you want the origin point. Press the SHIFT+S key and choose "Cursor to Selected" to align the 3D Cursor with the selection.

After you have the 3D Cursor aligned, go back to Object Mode and using the **Object → Set Origin → Origin to 3D Cursor** menu you can move the origin point to the same location as the 3D Cursor (Figure 3.7).

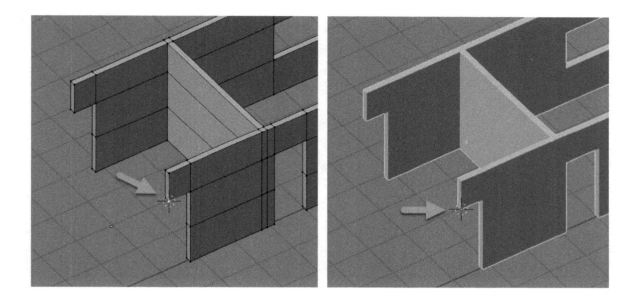

Figure 3.7 - *Origin point location*

With the origin point location set, we can easily apply the mirror. Add the Mirror modifier to the object and choose an axis. After you set the axis, Blender will make the mirrored copy from the object (Figure 3.8).

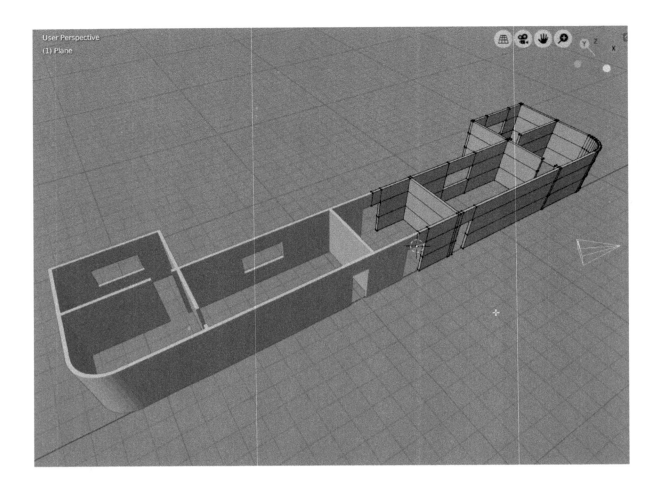

Figure 3.8 - *Mirrored copy*

The mirrored copy will share all the changes you make to the original object. For instance, you can go back and keep adding new elements like walls, and they will appear in the mirror.

If you want to make the copy "real" and make an independent geometry, you can apply the modifier. At the top of your Mirror modifier, you will find a button called "Apply" that will turn the mirror copy into an independent object.

Info: Keep in mind that after pressing that button you will no longer share any changes made to the object in just one of the sides.

3.3 Using repeating patterns for architectural modeling

Another common feature of architectural designs is the use of a pattern to define all shapes for a building. For instance, you could have a "block" with walls, windows, ornaments, and more. From that "block," you would repeat them several times to form a more massive structure.

Since that is a common feature of architecture, we could use the same technique in 3D modeling to make large models incredibly fast. All you have to do is make the pattern you want to use for repetition.

For instance, we can use the following pattern with a wall and window shown in Figure 3.9.

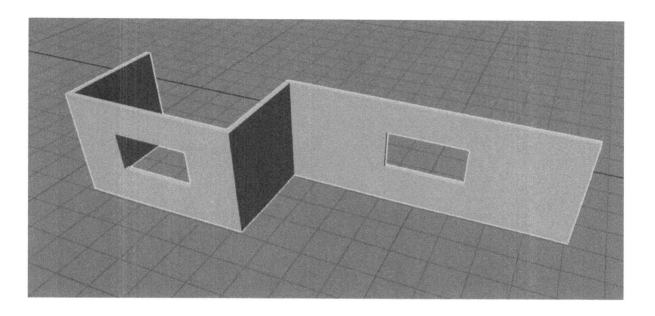

Figure 3.9 - Pattern for repetition

To copy that object and cover large surfaces, we will use the Array modifier, which is at the same location as the Mirror. At the Properties Editor in the Modifiers tab, you will find the Array. Just select the object and add the modifier (Figure 3.10).

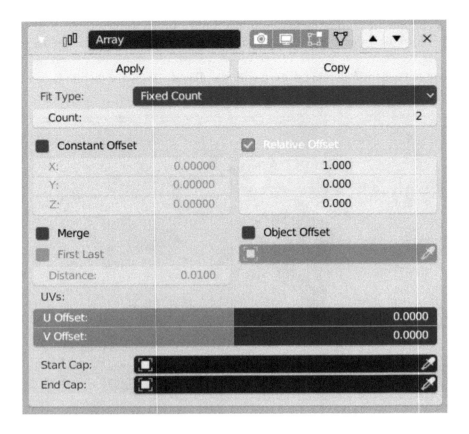

Figure 3.10 - *Modifier options*

From the modifier options, you will see two main methods for making copies:

- **Constant Offset**: Here you will use a fixed length for each copy, regardless of their size.
- **Relative Offset**: If you want to focus on how many copies you need instead of a length, you should use this option.

By choosing the Relative Offset option, you will have to pick how many copies you want and the axis. For instance, using a total of five copies in the X-axis will create the result shown in Figure 3.11.

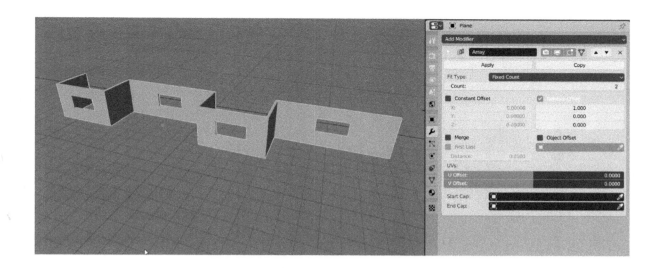

Figure 3.11 - *Copies in the X-axis*

If you change the axis to Z, they will stack on top of each other. What if we want to make a large wall using X and Z at the same time?

In that case, you will need two modifiers, one for each axis. Add another Array and set the bottom modifier to use seven copies in the Z-axis. The result will be a large stack of wall blocks to quickly build a much more complex model (Figure 3.12).

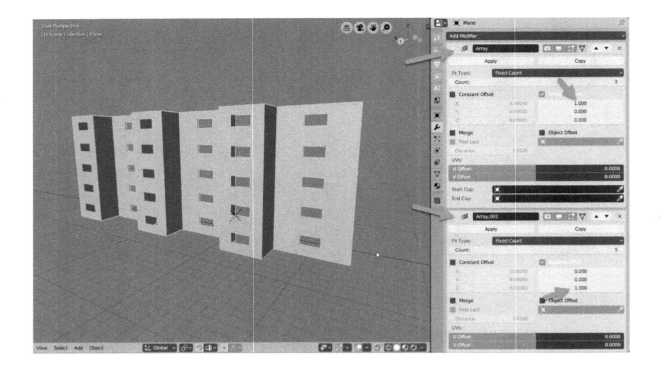

Figure 3.12 - Stack of blocks

You can apply the modifier to turn all copies in real 3D geometry, which will make you lose the main benefit of the pattern repetition. All changes applied to the original object will replicate to all copies.

Tip: You can remove modifiers from any object by pressing the X button on the top right corner of each modifier panel.

3.4 Composing shapes for architecture

An architectural model could have a lot of shapes that could be challenging to make in 3D, and depending on the tools available, might require you to come up with creative solutions. For instance, you could have a window shaped like a circle that is not easy to make using only an extrude.

In Blender, we have a modifier that can help to make such types of composing shapes called Boolean. With the Boolean modifier, you can use multiple forms to create a new one.

Here are the different types of Boolean operations available:

- **Difference**: You will subtract the shape of an object from another one
- **Intersect**: A new model will appear based on the intersection of two 3D models

– **Union**: A more substantial model will appear based on the union of two existing models

From all those options, you might want to pay close attention to the Difference. How does it work? We can use the example of a wall that needs a circular opening for a window.

To use a Boolean operation, you will have to make the wall model and also a cylinder that have the same size and proportions of the window. Make it a little thicker than the wall. You must place the cylinder at the exact location you wish for the window (Figure 3.13).

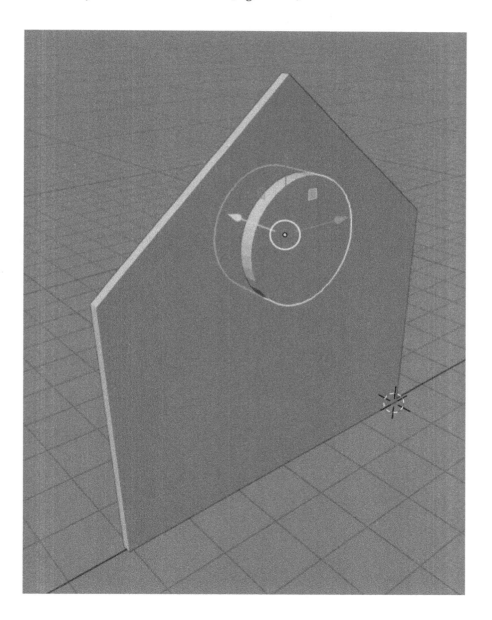

Figure 3.13 - *Wall and Cylinder*

Add the Boolean modifier to the wall model and choose Difference as the primary operation. At the Object field, you will have to inform the name of your cylinder object or use the eyedropper to pick the object (Figure 3.14) manually.

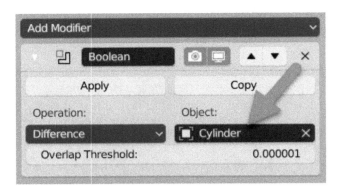

Figure 3.14 - *Boolean modifier*

At first, you won't see an immediate visual result of the operation because both the wall and cylinder will remain the same. However, if you hit the "Apply" button and move the cylinder away, the hole will appear in your wall (Figure 3.15).

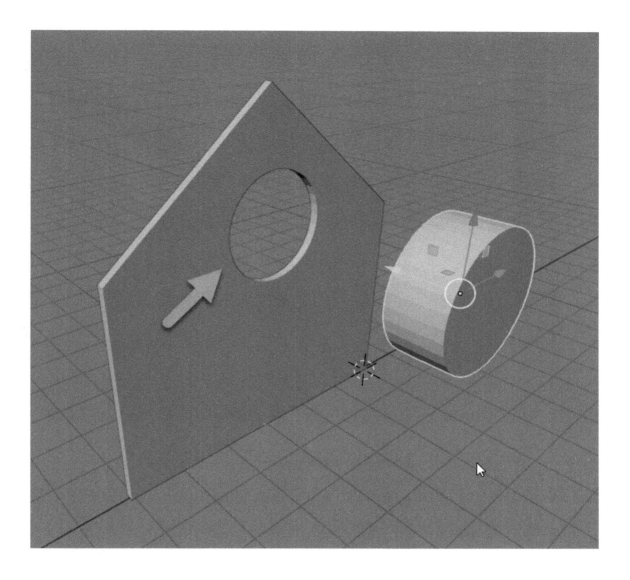

Figure 3.15 - *Wall with a circular hole*

You can also check to see if the operation worked by either pressing the Z key to view your models in wireframe mode or deleting the cylinder.

3.5 Profile-based modeling

If you want to make architectural details for models, a tool to create shapes based on profiles will be a great help. What is a profile? In that type of modeling, you will get a 2D shape and use it to build a larger shaped based on a path. It works like an extrude along a path.

A better way to demonstrate the technique is to look at Figure 3.16.

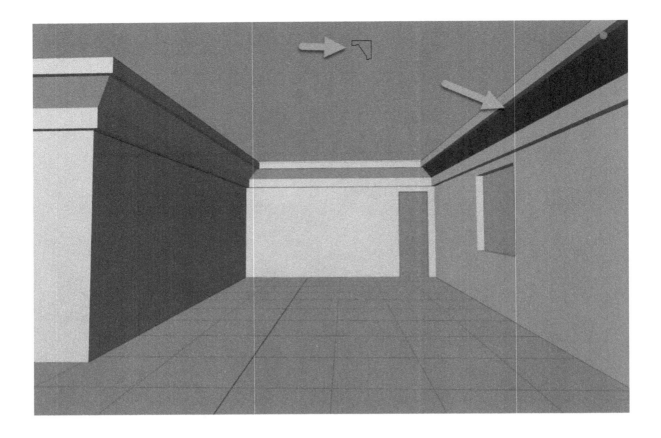

Figure 3.16 - *Profile-based modeling*

Look how we got a 2D profile of a shape and based on that form, we build a larger and more complex model.

In Blender, we can make that type of model using an option from a particular kind of object called curve. We will have to convert and objects between Mesh and Curves.

You will need two things to make 3D models based on profiles:

– A path that defines the full length of your model

– A 2D shape that will work as a reference for the model

Both objects must be curves in Blender. Instead of learning to manage and manipulate curves, we can start from a Mesh and convert that to a curve.

For instance, we can use the model shown in Figure 3.17 as an example. At the top of the walls, we can add a plaster detail surrounding the whole room.

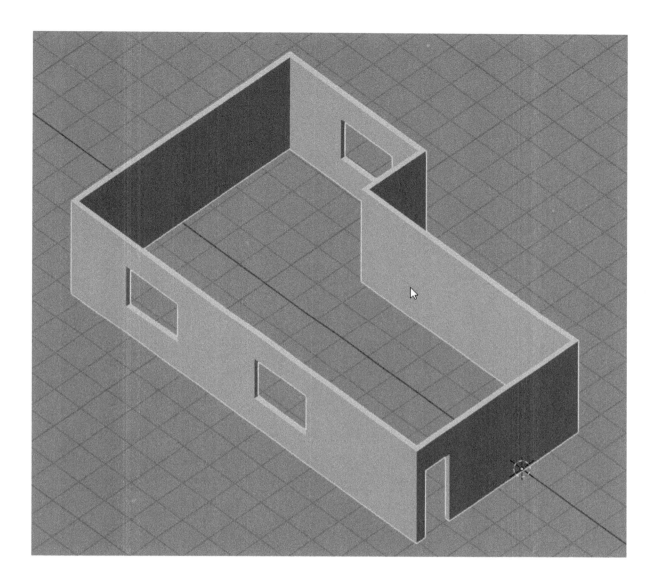

Figure 3.17 - *Room with walls for modeling*

The first thing you will need is the path to use for the modeling. Since we have our walls ready, you can use them to make the path quickly. Select one vertex from each corner of the wall and use the SHIFT+D key to duplicate them in the Z-axis (Figure 3.18).

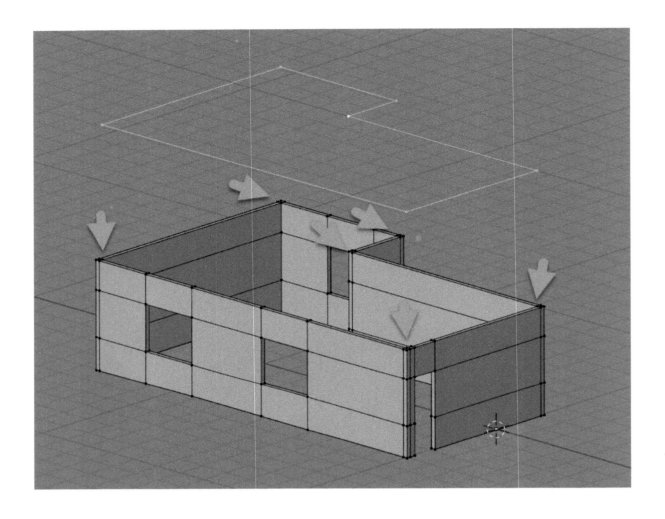

Figure 3.18 - Duplicating edges

Using the F key you can select two vertices and connect them with an edge. Connect all of them. Use the P key to separate the path.

You could also start from scratch and make the path using an extrude, but we can take advantage of existing geometry in this case.

The second step is to make our profile using a mesh object. You can use several tools and options to create a profile. A quick way to make it would be using a plane and a combination of extrudes, Loop Cuts and transformation to vertices get to the shape shown in Figure 3.19.

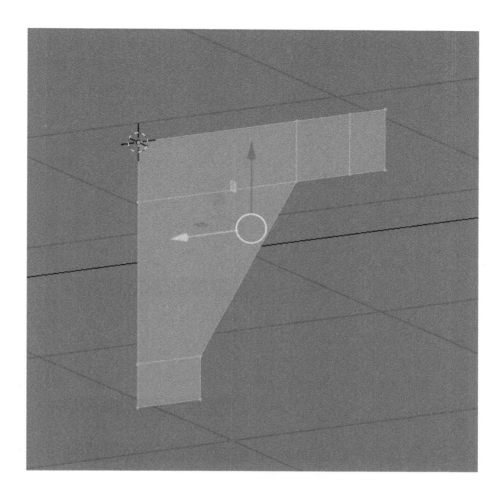

Figure 3.19 - *Profile for plaster detail*

Something critical for this type of modeling is the location of the origin point for the 2D profile. Look at Figure 3.19 and notice the origin location. It is at that so important? Because Blender will use that location as the reference to place the shape concerning the path.

With both the path and 2D shape ready, we can convert them both to curves. Go to the **Object → Convert to → Curve from Mesh/Text** menu. Nothing will happen visually, but both objects are now curves.

Select the path object and go to the Properties editor to open the Object Data tab. There you will see the options to edit and manipulate curves. Scroll down until you find the "Geometry" section and the Bevel options (Figure 3.20).

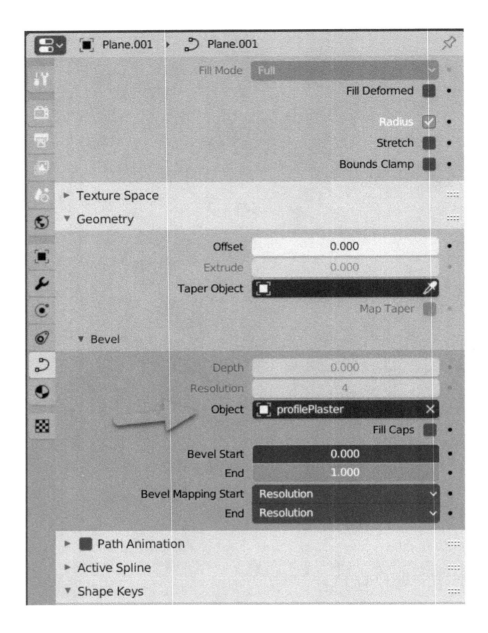

Figure 3.20 - Bevel options

At the Bevel options, we can choose in the Object field the 2D profile for our modeling. Choose the object based on their name or use the eyedropper to pick the shape manually. The result will be a new 3D object that will work like an "extrude along a path" (Figure 3.21).

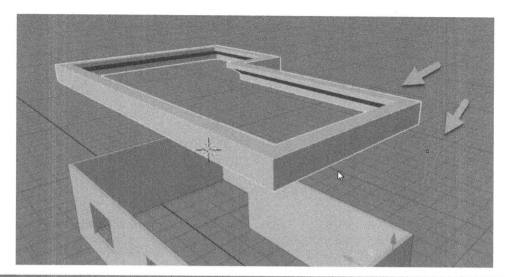

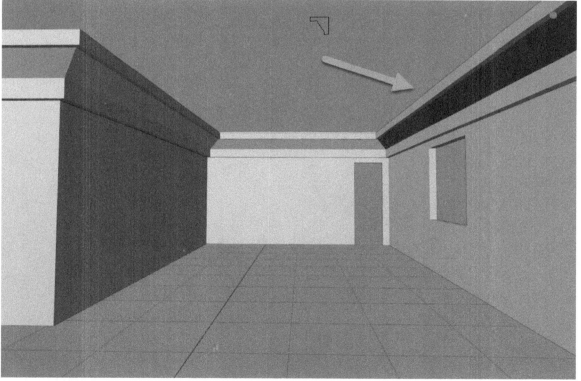

Figure 3.21 - *Extrude along a path?*

Since curve objects don't share the same features of meshes, we can convert the resulting object back to a mesh. With the object still selected, go to the **Object → Convert to → Mesh from Curve/Meta/Surf/Text** menu. That will turn the object back to a mesh.

3.6 Add-ons for modeling in architecture

Some elements of an architectural model could require a lot of time to create if you don't have the right tools. For instance, a wall that requires window frames and also doors. Those are the types of elements that could consume a significant amount of time to create.

Wouldn't be great to have something in Blender that could instantly create such objects?

Luckily, we will find in the Add-ons list of Blender an option to create such objects. What are Add-ons? Those are third-party scripts that anyone can write and use alongside Blender. Blender already has some of them bundled.

To see a list of all available Add-ons you can go to the **Edit → Preferences...** menu and choose the Add-ons tab. There you will see a list of all available scripts. Using the search box, you can type "Archimesh" to look for a particular script specialized in architecture (Figure 3.22).

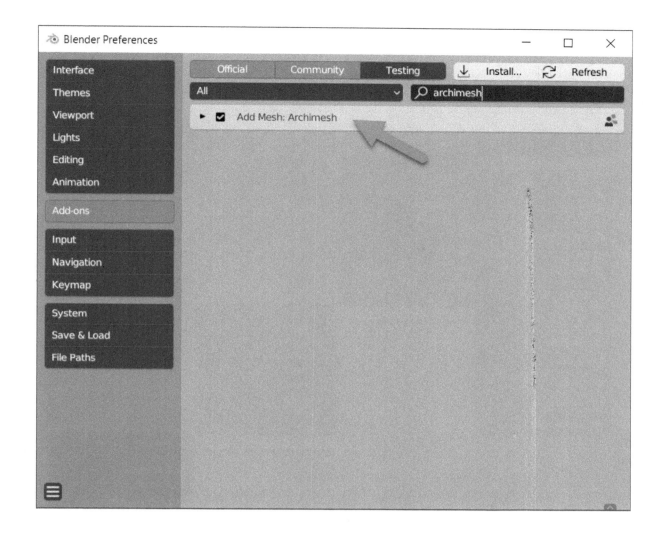

Figure 3.22 - Archimesh Add-on

Once you find the Add-on, you must enable it marking the small checkbox to the left of their name, and a new option will appear in your Add menu.

Now, if you press SHIFT+A and go to the Mesh group, you will see the Archmesh at the bottom. There you can see a list with all the options to create:

- Doors

- Rail windows

- Panel windows

- Shelves

– Stairs

Those are just a few of the options available (Figure 3.23).

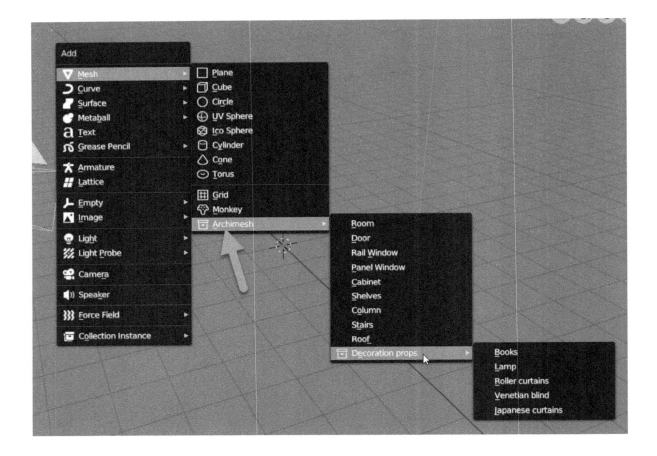

Figure 3.23 - *Archimesh options*

You will be able to save an incredible amount of time using the Add-on for modeling tasks and populating an architectural model with doors, windows, and more.

Info: Unfortunately, you won't be able to use and work with Imperial units using Archimesh. The Add-on still doesn't support that type of units.

3.7 Making windows

When you have to add a window model to a project related to architecture you have the option to make such object from scratch, which would demand a significant amount of time or use an Add-on like Archmesh. The Add-on will allow you to add several types of windows with just a few clicks.

From the Add-on menu, you will be able to add two main types of windows:

- Panel window

- Rail window

You can create them with the SHIFT+A key and use the **Mesh → Archimesh**. After you add each one of those window types, you can press the N key and go to the properties tab to edit and change details about the object.

Info: Remember to enable the Archimesh Add-on, or you won't see the options in your Add menu.

3.7.1 Adding Rail Windows

To create a Rail window for your projects, you must press the SHIFT+A key and choose that type of object from the **Mesh → Archimesh** group. After you add the model to your projects, you will see the result, as shown in Figure 3.24.

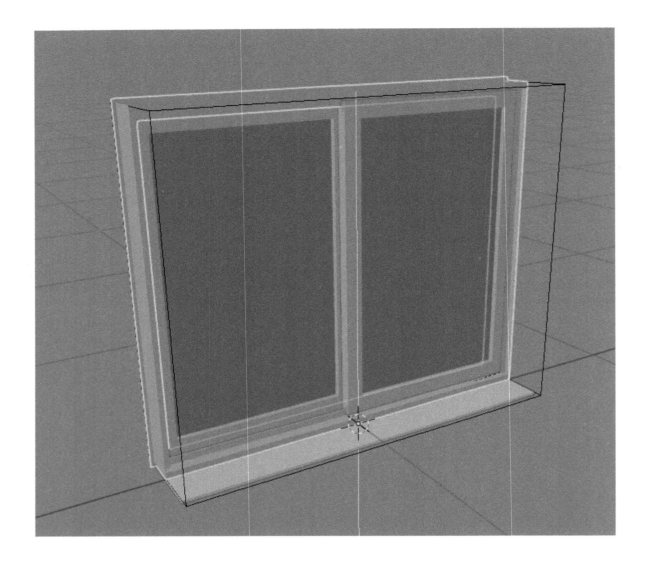

Figure 3.24 - *Rail window*

Open the properties tab with the N key and go to the Create section to edit and change settings for the window. There you will see a lot of options to change an edit aspects of your window (Figure 3.25).

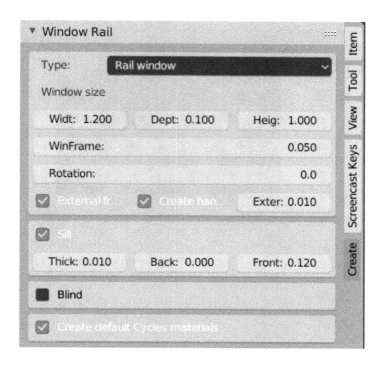

Figure 3.25 - Properties tab

At the Window rail section, you will be able to change the type of your window with four options Rail, Two leaf, Right leaf, and Left leaf. At the Window size, you get to change aspects like width, height, and thickness of your object (Figure 3.26).

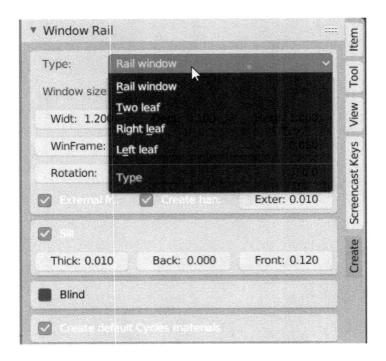

Figure 3.26 - *Window options*

You can even add a Blind to the window to make it look more appealing for interiors. As a plus, you also get Cyles materials for all the models. Since Cycles shares the same settings with Eevee, those materials will work on both renderers.

Tip: If you have to select and move windows from Archimesh, use the Empty at the bottom of each object.

3.7.2 Addind Panel windows

The panel windows will give you a lot more options regarding shapes and archetypes of objects for your projects. You will add them to the project using the same procedure, where you press the SHIFT+A key and choose the Panel window from the Archmesh menu.

At the properties tab, you will see a significant amount of customization options for that window type (Figure 3.27).

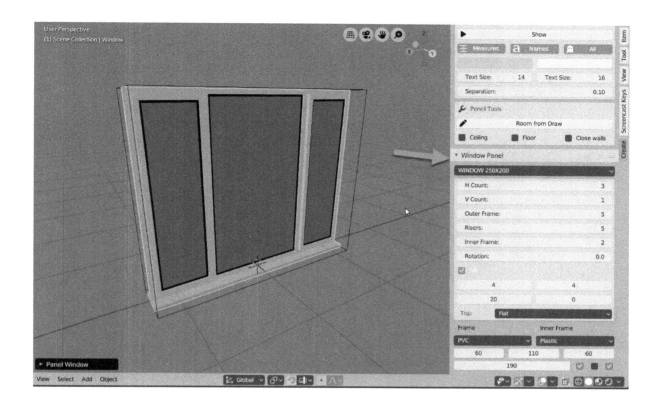

Figure 3.27 - *Panel window options*

A few things will catch your attention first like the ready to use dimension templates at the top of your options. There you can quickly pick options like 200x250 or 180x160 window frames. Since those are all based on glass, you can also use a template to make doors (Figure 3.28).

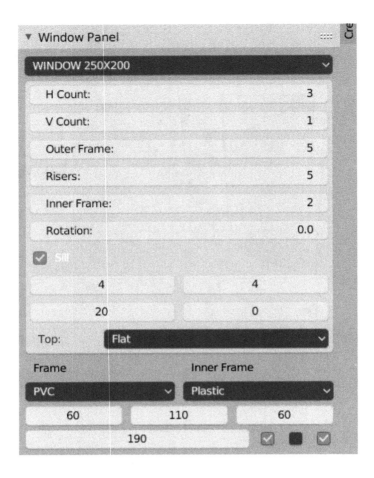

Figure 3.28 - *Window templates*

At the top, you have the freedom to set the number of divisions for your window using the H Count and V Count values.

Besides a traditional squared frame for your windows and doors, you can also choose other options for the top of your window. For instance, you can get an arch as the shape for the top or triangle (Figure 3.29).

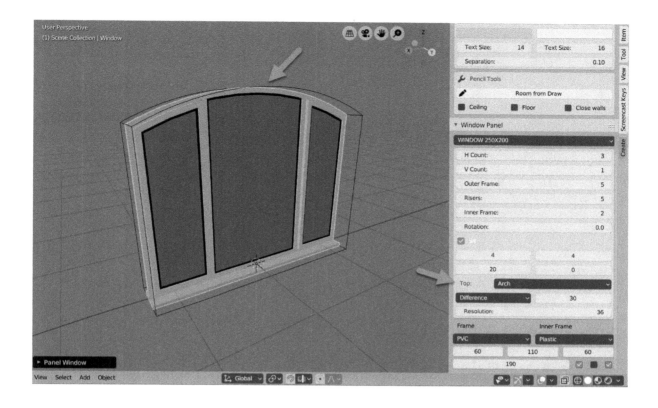

Figure 3.29 - Top options for windows

Regarding materials for the window, we even have the opportunity to get settings for three types of materials from PVC, Wood, or Plastic. For the outer or inner frame.

3.8 Adding doors to interior models

If you need a traditional door model for interiors, you can also make one using Archmesh. After you add the model to the scene, go to the properties tab to change settings for the door (Figure 3.30).

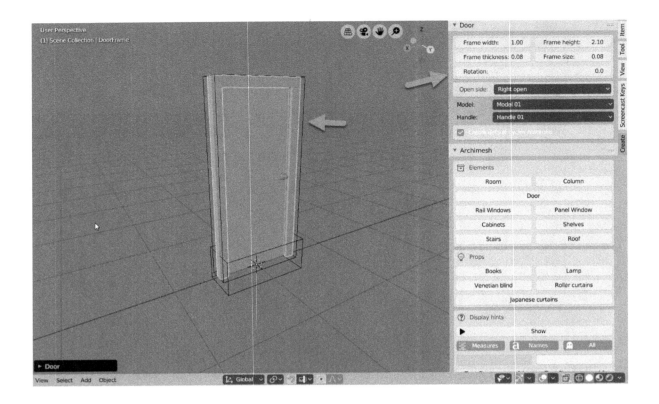

Figure 3.30 - *Door options*

At the options, you can change aspects of your door like Frame height, Frame width, and more. You can even set a rotation and choose the direction in which the door will open.

For instance, you can make a double door using the "Both sides" option (Figure 3.31).

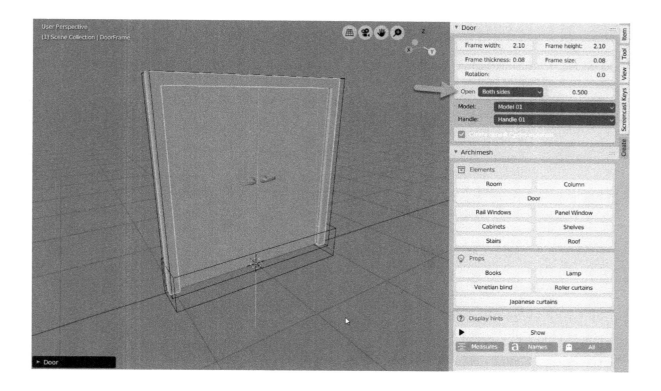

Figure 3.31 - *Double side door*

The bottom options will allow you to pick from several different types of door templates and handlers. For doors using glass, you should add a Panel window and change the template to the door type.

What is next?

We have a solid understanding of how to make architectural models in Blender at this point, but we have something missing. How to deal with technical drawings or other references in Blender? The next chapter will show how to use references for modeling in architecture.

You will learn how to process and import data to Blender from tools like AutoCAD, Revit, and others. Can Blender import DWG or DXF files? You will learn in the next chapter.

Another type of reference that we can use are image-based guides for modeling. You will see how to add and adjust their scale for architecture.

Chapter 4 - Modeling from CAD files and references

The design process of an architectural model will require you an excellent level of numeric precision when you decide to make all steps of the design in Blender. However, in some cases, you may receive or have a design coming from another tool. You can even receive data from someone else that needs a 3D model from a technical drawing.

In this chapter, you will learn how to manage and process references for modeling. From CAD files and how to prepare them to use in Blender to image references.

Here is a summary of what you will learn:

— Know how Blender handle CAD data

— Convert DWG and DXF files to use in Blender

— Enable Add-ons in Blender

— Prepare a technical drawing reference for modeling

— Use the snap with a technical drawing

— Add image references in the Viewport

— Create 3D models based on image references

4.1 Importing CAD files to Blender

Usually, when you start an architectural model in Blender, it will come from somewhere else as a final design. It could be from a CAD tool or a more advanced option like a BIM software. Regardless of where the plan started, you will want to get that model in 3D as fast as possible in Blender.

When you have a BIM tool, it will be easier because, by default, all designs start with 3D models. However, if you get a 2D drawing in popular formats like DWG or DXF, you have to find a way to import them to Blender.

How to import those models to Blender? If you open the **File → Import** menu in Blender, you will see all options available to import (Figure 4.1).

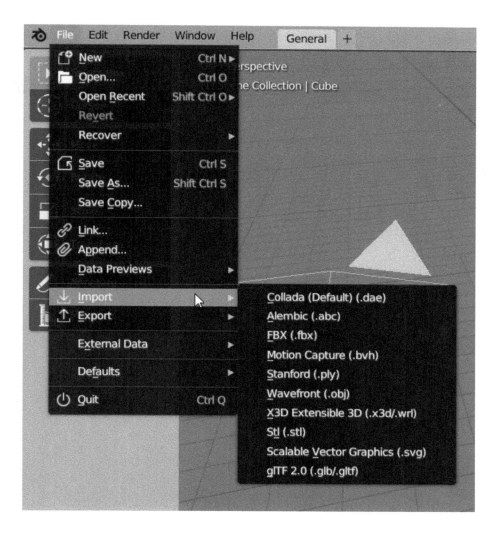

Figure 4.1 - *Blender import options*

At first, you won't see anything that could help us working with CAD data.

If you have access to the source file where the design came, it would be a great idea to export the data to either FBX or OBJ. Both of those files will work great with Blender and doesn't require much processing.

What if you don't have access to the source files and software? In this case, we will have to convert and process the data to get it to Blender. Blender can import DXF files with the use of an Add-on.

It may not appear in the file menu by default, which will require you to enable the Add-on. Go to the **Edit → Preferences...** menu and open the Add-ons tab. Type DXF in the search box, and you will see two options. One for export and another to import files (Figure 4.2).

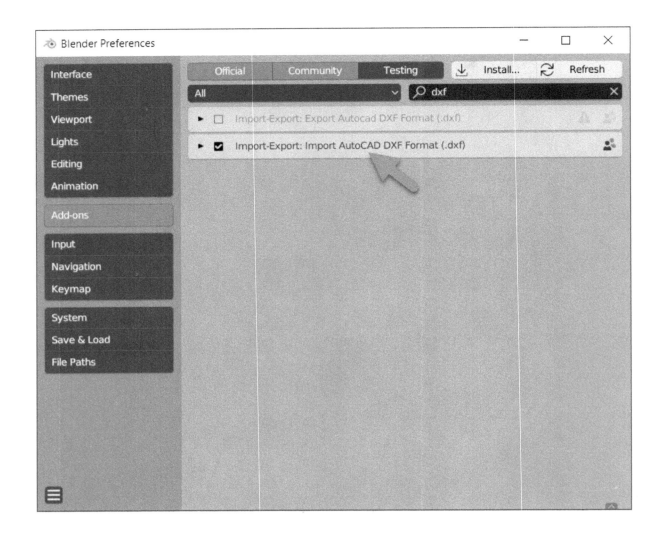

Figure 4.2 - DXF import to Blender

After you enable the option to import DXF files, you will see it in the File menu (Figure 4.3).

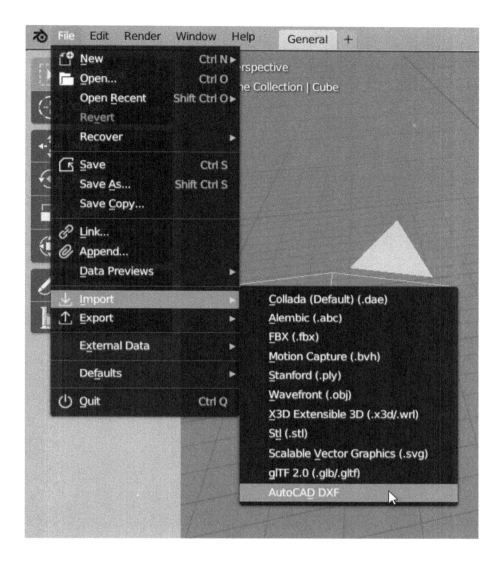

Figure 4.3 - DXF import

That will solve the problem of importing DXF files to Blender, but we still need another common type of file for our projects. Can we import DWG files? Very few tools can handle DWG files besides AutoCAD and Blender is among the ones that can't open such files.

The solution would be to convert the DWG files to DXF!

4.2 Converting CAD files for better compatibility

Even with a native option in Blender to importing DXF files, you may experience problems when trying to import specific files. The reason for that is because you will find versions for both DXF and DWG files. For instance, a newer version of the DXF file could not be compatible with the Blender Add-on.

To overcome that problem, we would have to convert the file to an older version to make it easier for Blender to import.

How to convert the files? There is a free tool that you should keep in hand from the Open Design Alliance that can transform and manage DXF and DWG files. With the ODA File Converter, you can change versions of DXF files and also convert DWG to DXF.

The software is not open-source like Blender, but a freeware that works on multiple systems including Windows, macOS, and Linux. To download the converter, you must visit this address:

– https://www.opendesign.com/guestfiles/oda_file_converter

If this URL doesn't work, you can search for the latest version of the ODA File Converter on your preferred search engine.

The installation process is straightforward and doesn't require anything special. Once you have the converter installed, open the software to see all options available. In Figure 4.4, you can see the primary user interface for the converter.

Figure 4.4 - *ODA File Converter*

One thing you should know about the converter is that it only works with the batch conversion of files. You will need to specify two folders on your computer:

– **Input folder**: For your DXF and DWG files

– **Output folder**: For the conversion results

What if you want to convert a single file? Place that file in the input folder, and you will get a single conversion.

Tip: Make a backup of your DWG and DXF files before you start performing multiple conversions.

The process to convert files is incredibly simple:

1. Choose the input and output folders

2. Make sure you have the source files in the input folder

3. Select an output version. For Blender, you can use DXF 2010 to ensure maximum compatibility

4. Press the "Start" button

That will work for both DWG and DXF files. If you check the output folder after you process the data, you will see them in DXF.

4.3 Importing and preparing CAD files for modeling

After you have the files in DXF format, it is time to import them to Blender. Go to the File menu and choose AutoCAD DXF to import your project. Since we will use the files for modeling reference, you can leave all options from the DXF dialog on the left in their default values (Figure 4.5).

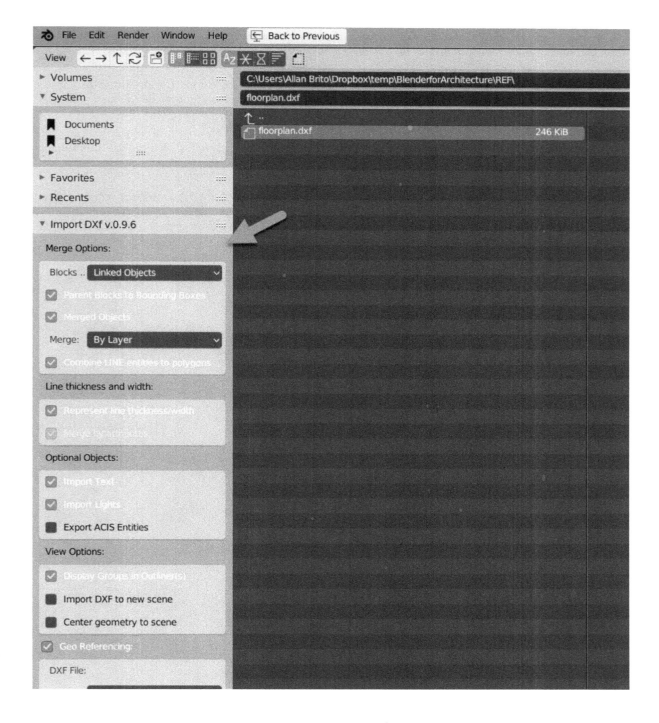

Figure 4.5 - *DXF options for importing*

Select the file and hit the Import DXF button on the top right. One thing that we could do to help is handling the scale conversion of the file.

Depending on the scale of the technical drawing you are importing from a DXF or DWG, you can get some massive geometry in your scene. That will depend on the scale used in the technical drawing.

For instance, if you know that a particular drawing is using centimeters for drawing, it means 1 meter will have 100 units in the drawing. Blender uses units that are more equivalent to meters, which will make a wall in your technical drawing with 1 meter have 100 units in Blender.

It might become confusing, making all those calculations for scaling. You can also make a more visual approach.

After you import a file, press the Home key, or use the **View → Frame All** menu. That will adjust the viewing angle of your scene to display everything. To ensure you are viewing everything, change the view to the top with the 7 key from the Numpad and also press the 5 key to use an orthogonal projection (Figure 4.6).

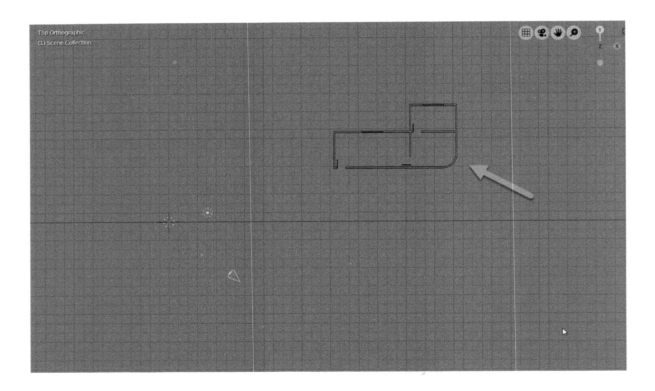

Figure 4.6 - Viewing all the drawing

If your drawing is too big, you can press the A key to select everything and using the S key, apply a scale to shrink it down. Do not apply a random scale with the mouse. Instead, use a more regular value like "0.1" to reduce the size by 90%.

However, if you think the scale is correct you don't have to apply any transformations.

116

4.3.1 Organising the drawing in collections

The next step is to remove all unnecessary information from the technical drawing. Since we will use the lines as a reference for modeling, you probably won't need a lot of the data from the technical drawing like dimension lines, text, and some blocks.

You can select the objects and delete them from the drawing. A few options in Blender could help you make that selection process a lot easier. Select only the lines you want to keep in the drawing and go to the **Select → Invert** menu. That will select everything you don't want and make it easier to remove them.

Once you have only the lines you want like all walls, it is time to place them in a protected collection to give you more freedom to model. The collections in Blender are similar to layers in a CAD software where you can make "groups" of data for manipulation.

With the walls selected, press the M key and choose the "New Collection" option from the menu. Pick a name for the objects like "reference." That will get the objects and place them in a new collection (Figure 4.7).

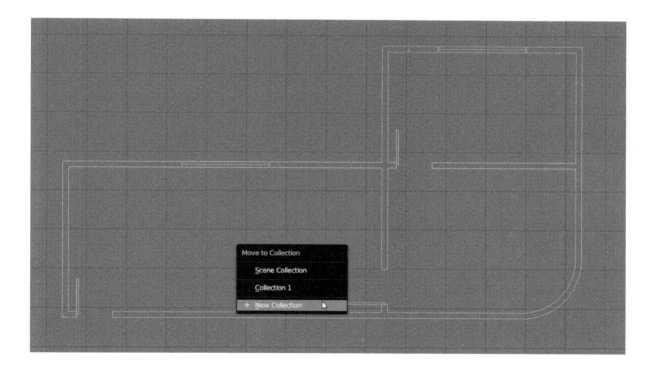

Figure 4.7 - *Objects in collection*

The collections will appear at the Outliner editor and will offer a convenient way to protect any drawing. Why do you need to protect the drawing?

Because once we start using it as a reference for modeling, you will want to use that as a background for a modeling project. And you don't want to select or change either the position or scale accidentally.

The Outliner editor offers a way to hide the object with the small eye icon right next to the collection name. To disable any selection, you have to select the Object tab in the Properties Editor and locate the Visibility options (Figure 4.8).

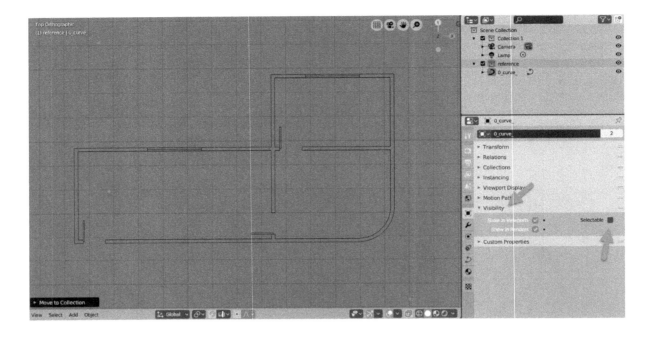

Figure 4.8 - Visibility options

There you can disable the Selectable, and your drawing will no longer be part of any selection or interact with the mouse.

How to turn on the Selectable option? Click on the collection name at the Outliner Editor, and you will be able to go back to the Visibility options to enable selections again.

A few points regarding collections:

- You can make as many collections as you like, use the M key in your Viewport or with a right-click inside the Outliner Editor choose the New option.
- You can create stacks of collections. Just click and drag a collection inside the Outliner to reorganize them.
- You can move objects between collections with the M key in the Viewport

4.4 Modeling from CAD files with the Snap

With a technical drawing in place and protected, we can start using it as a reference for modeling. Using a technical drawing with vector data is one of the fastest ways to speed up modeling in architecture because you will only have to follow the lines with the snap to get a model ready.

In Blender, we can use the Snap During Transform option to help us during modeling. You will enable the option with the small magnet icon in the Viewport header. The shortcut for the tool is SHIFT+TAB.

Enable the tool and from their options, which is available in the button right next to the magnet. Choose the Vertex as the main element and for the Target pick the "Closest" (Figure 4.9).

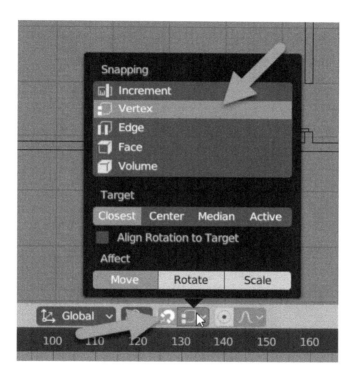

Figure 4.9 - *Snap during transform*

By choosing those options, you will:

- Capture all vertices from objects during a transform operation like moving, rotating, and scaling.
- It will be the closest vertices to the mouse cursor

The next step is to add a plane to the scene and start working on the modeling. Since we have the snap enabled, you can move the cursor with the G key until it captures a vertex from the technical drawing (Figure 4.10).

119

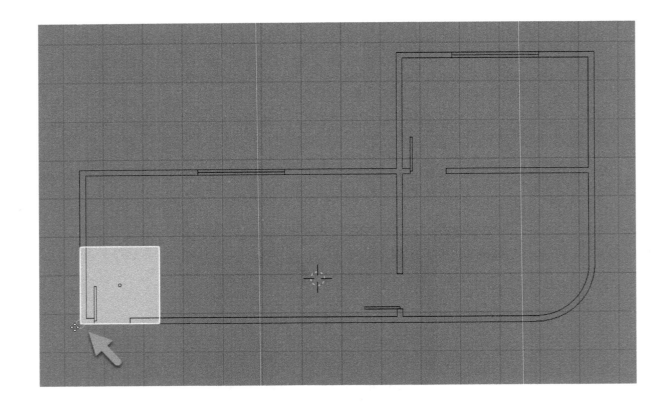

Figure 4.10 - *Capturing a vertex*

You will see a small circle that will give you visual feedback on what vertex the snap is capturing.

Go to Edit Mode for the plane and select only the top vertices of your plane, and move them in the Y-axis and the X-axis until you align the plane with the wall thickness (Figure 4.11).

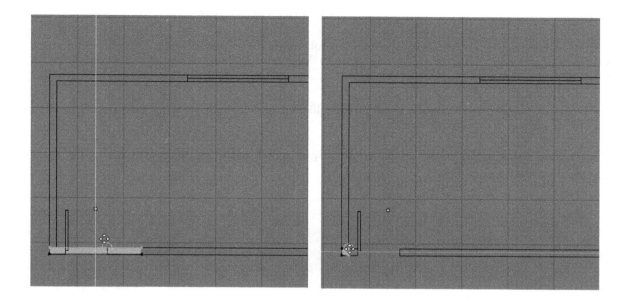

Figure 4.11 - *Adjusting the plane to the wall*

You can use the G key, Y key, and X key for that operation.

Change the selection mode do edge, and select the edge showed in Figure 4.12. Move that edge until you reach the vertex marking the start point of a window.

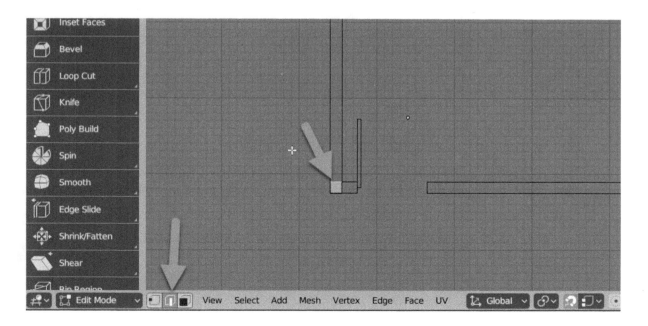

Figure 4.12 - *Selected edge*

From that edge, you can start using the extrude tool to build the rest of all walls. Press the E key and the corresponding axis key to make all extrude. Keep making extrudes and use the snap to capture reference points quickly.

If you have to make interruptions to the extrude, like when you reach the space for a door you can use a SHIFT+D instead to duplicate the edge.

After a few extrudes, you will be able to get the full model with walls (Figure 4.13). You can use the Spin tool to make the curved wall.

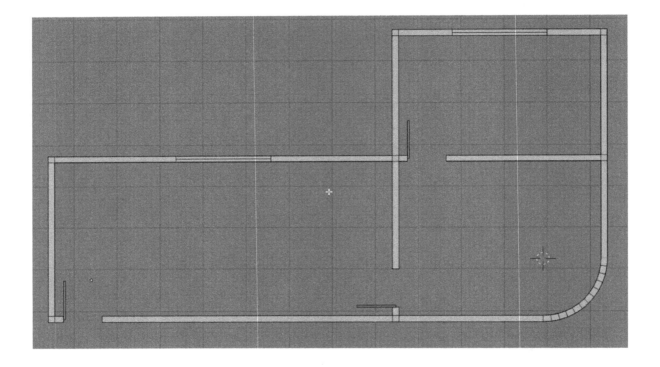

Figure 4.13 - *Model with all walls*

That is by far the fastest way to make architectural models in Blender because you won't have to type any numeric values to build your 3D model. Everything will come from the existing technical drawing reference.

For that reason, you should always use a technical drawing as a reference for drawing if you have one available for the project.

4.5 Importing references for modeling

A technical drawing is an excellent reference for any architectural visualization project where you have to create a 3D model from something like a floorplan. However, in some case, you won't have at your disposal a technical drawing as a DXF or DWG file. Some professionals will eventually receive a PDF or worse to use as a reference.

For instance, you could receive an image file like a PNG or JPG to use as a reference for all your modeling. You have the technical drawing, but not in vector shape. That will make it hard to use tools like the Snap During Transform in Blender.

Even with no vector data, we can still use the material as a reference for modeling in architecture. It won't be as precise like a technical drawing in vector model, but it could also help in the modeling stage.

If you have a PDF file, you will need to convert that to an image like a PNG or JPG.

In Blender, we can import and use images to place in the Viewport to aid in modeling. To get an image to the Viewport, you will first change the view you have from the scene to top, using the 7 key of your Numpad.

At the top view, you will press the SHIFT+A key and choose the **Image → Reference** option (Figure 4.14).

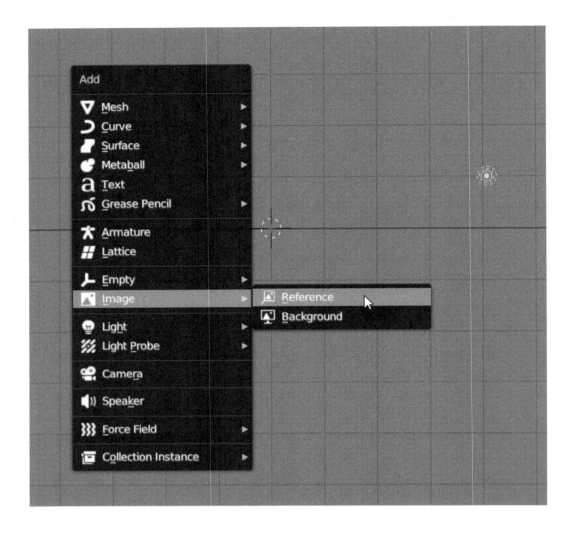

Figure 4.14 - Reference image

Blender will prompt you to select the image you wish to use. Make sure you keep the "Align to view" option marked on the left and choose the image you want.

For instance, we can get the image of a floorplan to use as a reference for modeling (Figure 4.15).

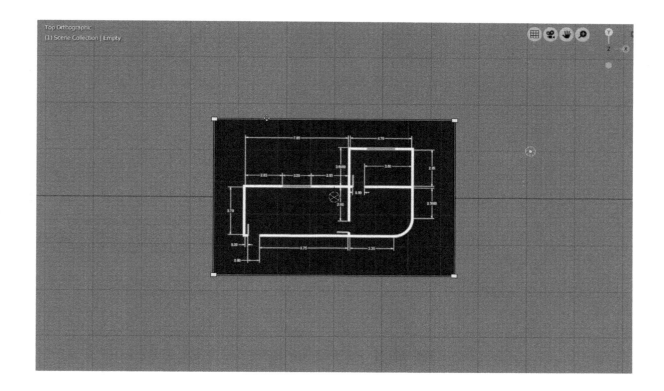

Figure 4.15 - *Floorplan as a reference*

The reference image will work as a 3D object in your scene, and you will be able to select it and apply any transformation tools. You can move, rotate, or scale the image if you need. At the corners of your image, you will see handlers that will make scaling operations even more straightforward.

By clicking and dragging from the handlers, you will be able to resize the images quickly.

To have even more control over your image, you can select the image and go to the Object Data tab in your Properties Editor (Figure 4.16).

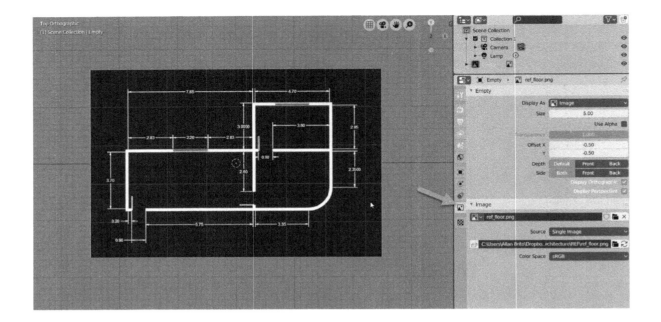

Figure 4.16 - *Reference image options*

There you will find:

– Numeric control for the image size

– A transparency slider to make your reference transparent. You must check the "Use Alpha" to make it work

– Options to display your image on both perspective and orthographic projections

Since we are using the image as a reference for modeling and to avoid any potential problems from getting a reference in perspective, you can disable the display on perspective projections.

Another critical adjustment you must perform to ensure you have a great reference image for modeling, is to disable the selection of your reference image. That will protect the image from accidental transformations during the modeling stage.

Select the image and open the Visibility options in the Object tab. The Object tab is part of the Properties Editor. There you will find the "Selectable" option that can disable.

You can reselect the object using the Outline Editor and clicking at the image name. After you select the object, go back to the Visibility options, and enable the selection again.

4.6 Scale adjustments for modeling

What about the scale? One of the advantages of using a technical drawing from a DWF or DWG is the benefit of having an accurate size. Unfortunately, you won't be able to get the same accuracy with an image.

However, we can make it get close to the actual scale for modeling. To do that we have to find the size of any part of your project based on the image. For instance, look at the wall pointed in Figure 4.17.

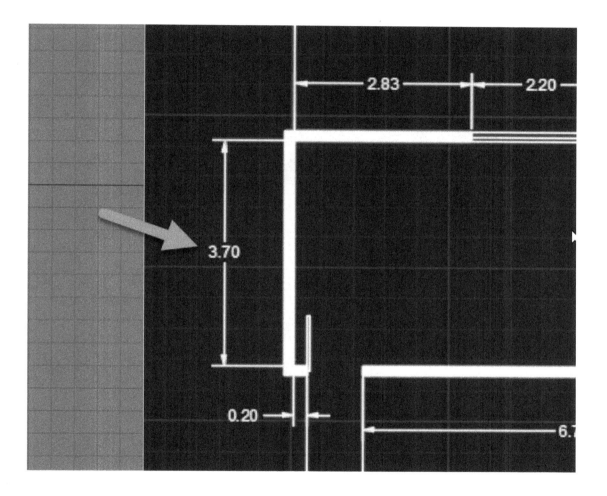

Figure 4.17 - *Wall from image*

From the dimension lines, you will see that this wall have 3.7 meters in length. What is the size of the wall in Blender? We will be able to get a close value by creating a reference object.

Add a plane to the scene, and in edit mode, you can erase two vertices from the plane to leave only a single edge. Resize that edge to match as close as possible the size of that wall. Enable the edge length display from the Overlays, and you will see value in Blender (Figure 4.18).

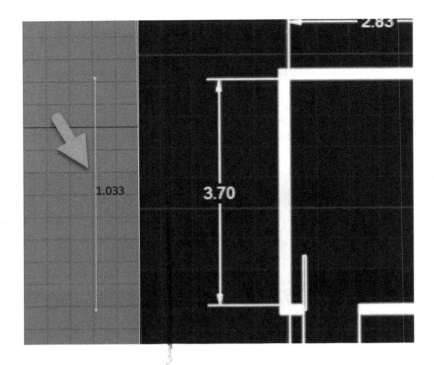

Figure 4.18 - Edge length

We have the edge with 1.033, and it should be 3.7. To find the scale factor you need for the image, you will get the desired length and divide by the actual size:

3.7 / 1.033 = 3.58

Select the image reference and using the S key apply a numeric scale with this factor. If you align the edge to the wall, they will have a very similar size. It won't be perfect, but close enough to produce a 3D model with the correct proportions.

4.7 Modeling based on image references

Having an image reference for modeling could not give you the same level of productivity and speed from a vector drawing. But, it will help nonetheless to get an architectural model created. You will have to leave behind a few details about the model.

The first thing you won't have is total accuracy on dimensions. All modeling will use visual references instead of exact measures. But, it will be good enough to have the project with the correct proportions.

Second, your main modeling procedure will only use the mouse cursor move to build all the geometry.

How to work with reference images? After you have the image in place and with the correct scale, we can start making the model. Add a plane, or any other object you like, and using the S key, adjust the size to fit a part of the image reference (Figure 4.19).

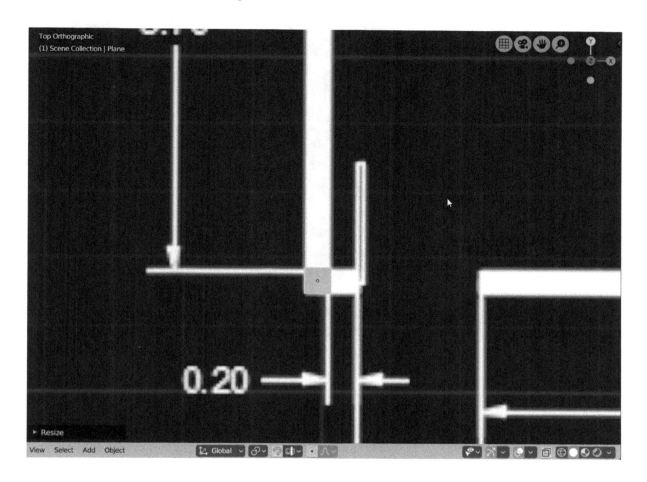

Figure 4.19 - *Adjust the first object scale*

At this point, it will be better to work with a shading mode like Wireframe. Press the Z key and choose that shading mode.

Go to Edit Mode and select an edge from the plane and with the G key and the correspondent axis keys, you will move the edges until they fit your reference (Figure 4.20).

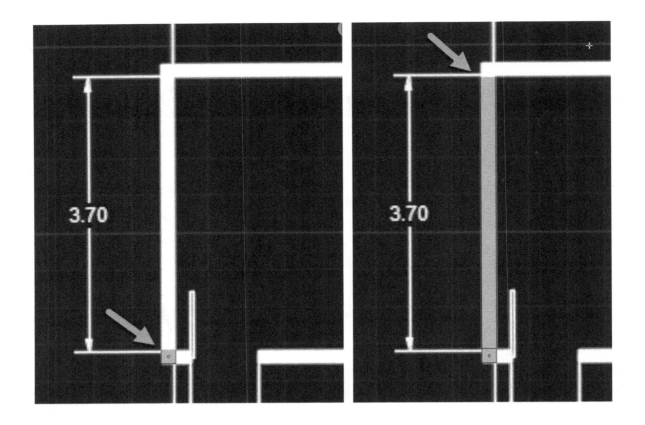

Figure 4.20 - *Adjusting the plane*

With the plane adjusted, we can start to use the extrude to build the rest of our walls. Remember that you can create gaps in the wall using a SHIFT+D instead of the extrude. Use the axis keys to constraint and keep all extrudes orthogonal (Figure 4.21).

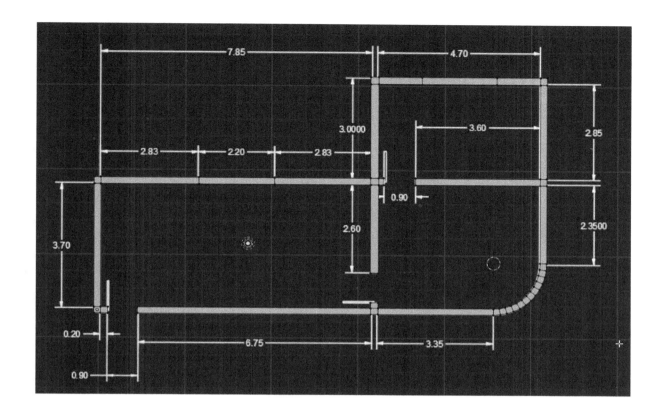

Figure 4.21 - *Walls from reference*

The model will have a proportion good enough to create all the visualization necessary for your project.

What is next?

The modeling of any architectural model will require from you a set of information and tools to quickly assemble a detailed and accurate 3D object. You know how to start modeling architectural elements using all kinds of resources, but we still have something missing from the projects.

We need furniture and assets to populate our designs and make a better visualization for the projects.

In the next chapter, you will learn how to manage and work with external assets in Blender, import furniture models, and prepare them to receive materials.

That is the next step we need to make better models for architecture in Blender.

Chapter 5 - Furniture and external assets

What would be of architectural projects in 3D with no assets in the scene? The use of assets like furniture models are essential to give a sense of scale to a virtual representation of a project, and also for context.

For instance, you can make a bunch of walls and architectural elements and still can't figure out the purpose of that space. After inserting desks and chairs, you probably will associate that to an office project. Add a sofa, and a table see that as a residential project.

Having furniture assets is part of any architectural modeling process. In this chapter, you will learn how to handle and deal with external libraries for furniture and assets in Blender.

Here is what you will learn:

– How to import assets to Blender

– Use the Append and Link options

– Working with linked external libraries

– Editing external libraries assets with furniture

– Optimizing and fixing furniture models

– Prepare furniture models for reuse in Blender

5.1 Handling external assets in Blender

Besides all architectural elements like walls, windows, doors, stairs, and other you will also have to deal with a significant amount of assets in a project. The most common type of asset for architectural projects are furniture models that could range from small objects for interiors to urban furniture.

No matter the type of furniture you will use for a particular project. It is imperative to learn all the tools and options regarding asset management in Blender to both save time and work in future projects.

Just like any other 3D tool and design software, you have quite a few options to reuse and exchange models between files to create personalized asset library. The tools in Blender will allow you to exchange all kinds of information, from 3D models to textures and materials.

Most of the data inside a Blender file is accessible using two unique options in the File menu called Append and Link. If you are familiar with the concept of XREF in design software, you will immediately notice how they work similarly.

5.1.1 Using the Append and Link

The way Blender uses to get data from external files is with two tools called Append and Link. Both of them appear at the File menu (Figure 5.1).

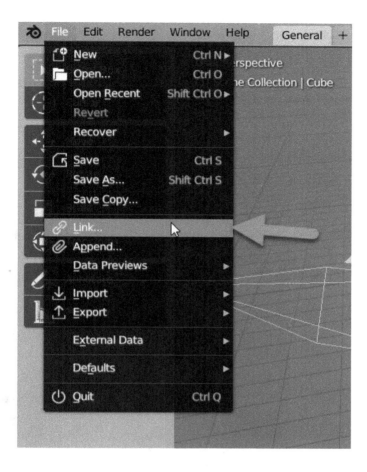

Figure 5.1 - File menu

Both the Append and Link works as an import option, but exclusively for Blender files. Once you pick any one of them, you will see the file selection screen where you must choose a Blender file.

What is the difference between an Append and Link? Here is how they work:

- **Append**: Will get data from external files and make a copy to your current project. No relation or connection to the source file. You can edit the contents inside your project.

- **Link**: Instead of making a copy of the data, you will insert a reference in your project. Most of the editing options won't be available since it is a reference to external data. You can apply transformations like move and scale. But most of the options will appear locked.

If you want to make a direct copy of a model or asset to a new project, you will probably want to use the Append option. It works as an import, but for Blender assets.

The Link will give you a more sophisticated reference to external material. It is excellent for projects where multiple people collaborate on a large project. You can have someone working in the primary 3D model and others updating assets or furniture.

Regardless of the method, you can bring data to your projects from other Blender files. After you choose a Blender file, you will see a lot of folders that have all the information from that particular project (Figure 5.2).

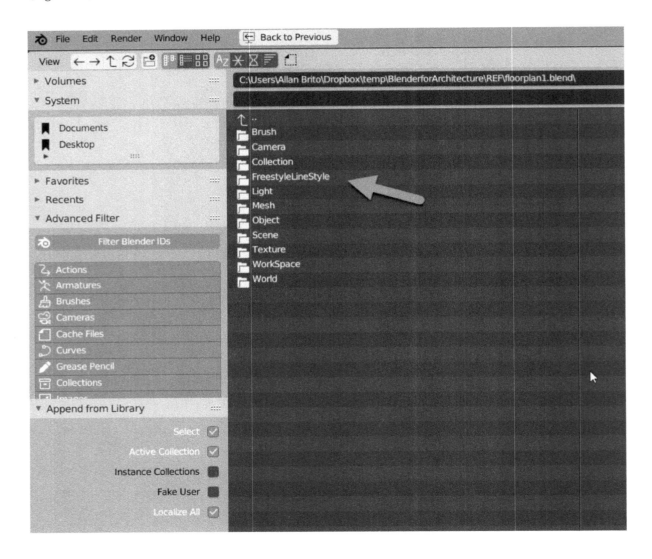

Figure 5.2 - *Folders in Blender file*

As you can see from Figure 5.2, the folders will organize the data in categories like:

- Object
- Material
- Texture
- Camera
- Mesh

To get a 3D model from that file and bring it to your current project, you must pick the Object folder. There you will see a list with the names of all objects on that file.

Here comes a situation where assigning unique and meaningful names to objects will make all the difference. Instead of having default names like "Cube.001", "Cylinder," and other you might get "Lounge-Chair" or anything else that helps you identify those models.

You can select one of the multiple objects from the list and hit the button "Append from Library" when you are ready.

Tip: Hold down the SHIFT key in the selection screen to get multiple objects.

5.2 Append furniture models from external files

The process of getting an external model to Blender is easy with the use of either an Append or Link. After you choose the file you want to use, go to the Object folder and get the names of all the assets you need.

For instance, we can get a particular chair model from the scene shown in Figure 5.3.

Figure 5.3 - *Interior Scene*

To make all process a lot easier, we will check the object name, which is easy to identify after selecting the object. The name is "ChaseChair" as you can see in Figure 5.4.

Figure 5.4 - Furniture model name

By the way, you can rename the model if you want using that same field in the Properties editor.

Another critical aspect of the process is to get an exact location for the Blender file and folder. Otherwise, you won't be able to get that from the Append and Link. The file name is "archscene.blend" and it is on the computers Desktop folder.

We can make a new scene in Blender and immediately go to the File menu and trigger the Append option. There you will navigate to the Desktop folder and find the file "archscene.blend" and inside the Object folder, you will get the "ChaseChair" model (Figure 5.5).

Figure 5.5 - Selecting the furniture model

After you press the "Append from Library" button, you will see the furniture model in your current scene in Blender. It is quite simple to get external files from other Blender files. You can edit and change all aspects of the 3D model in the new scene file.

What if we use the Link option?

The main difference with the use of a Link is that you won't be able to edit a lot of details about the furniture model. For instance, your Object editor appear with all options disabled (Figure 5.6).

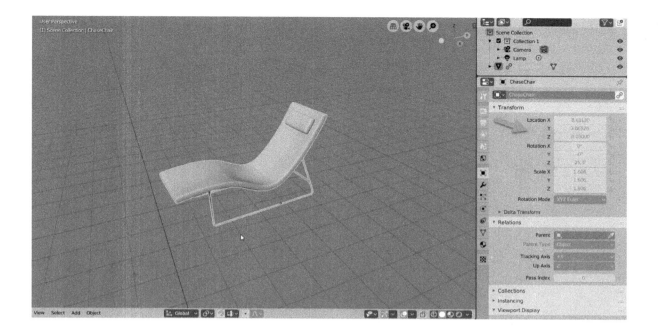

Figure 5.6 - Using assets with a Link

Besides that, you have to take a few precautions when using a link:

- Make sure you won't have to move or rename the file you are linking. Otherwise, you might lose the connection to the object

- Save the file you are editing in Blender before using the link. That way you will get absolute links to the original object

- Any changes you apply to the original file will propagate to all scene using the assets with a link

There are a few projects where you will want to use a link to keep a consistent library, but in most cases, an Append will be enough.

5.3 Proxy objects for linked models

For every asset that you add in a project using the Link option, you will have to follow a few steps to update and change details about the model. At first, even fundamental aspects of handling the model won't be available like simple transformations like move, rotate, and scale.

The solution to edit and manipulate linked objects is to make a proxy in your Blender file. What is a proxy? A proxy works like an empty object that controls the linked model. You will be able to apply transformations and other minor editing procedures to the proxy, but not to the linked object.

In the Outliner Editor, you will see the proxy listed with the same name of your linked object with a suffix "_proxy." How to create a proxy?

You have first to select the object linked to an external Blender file, like a furniture model. Go to the **Object → Relations → Make Proxy…** to make a proxy of your model (Figure 5.7).

Figure 5.7 - Making a proxy

The main benefit of using a proxy will be the ability to edit and transform the object copy. A few actions you can take with a proxy:

- Apply transformations

- Use modifiers for copying

- Duplicate the object and proxy

Even with a proxy, you can't make direct changes to objects materials or polygon structure.

5.3.1 Editing external files in Blender

The traditional way of editing linked objects in Blender is to open the original file and make the necessary changes. There you will save the file, and all changes propagate to any scenes using linked objects.

What if you have to make a quick change to an asset in a project? Is there a way to make such changes without the need to open the original file?

There is an Add-on that can help with that task. With the "Edit Linked Library" Add-on you have a convenient way to edit any linked file without the need to open another Blender instance.

First, you have to enable the Add-on in the **Edit → Preferences...** menu in the Add-ons tab. There you can use the search box to find the Add-on quickly. Just type "Linked," and you will see the Add-on (Figure 5.8).

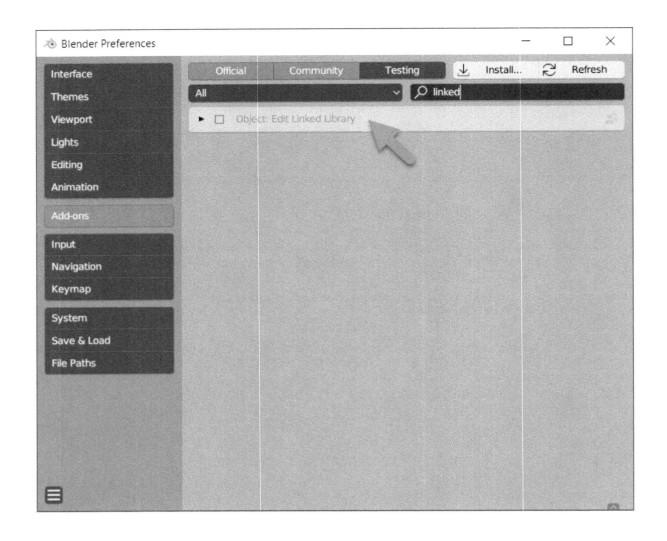

Figure 5.8 - *Edit Linked Library*

After you enable the Add-on, a new option will appear in the Properties tab. Select an object that is in your scene with a link, and you will see the "Edit Library" button (Figure 5.9).

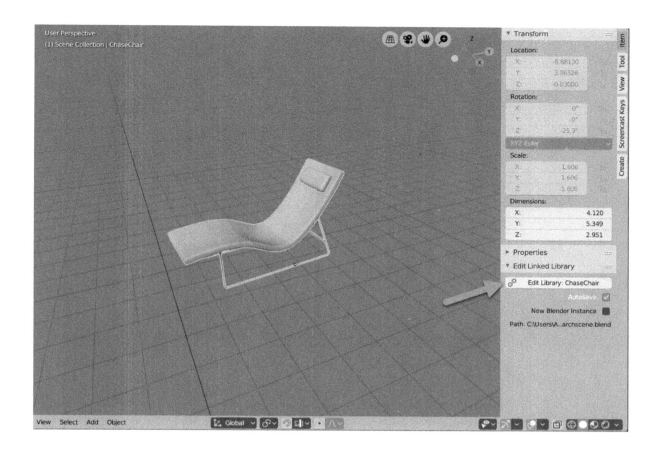

Figure 5.9 - *Edit Library*

Once you click on this button, Blender will try to open the original file and give you full access to edit any characteristic of the model you want. Notice that it opens the source file. When you finish the editing process, save the file, and at the Properties tab, you will find a button "Return to Original File" (Figure 5.10).

Figure 5.10 - *Return to file*

Press this button, and you will go back to the original file with all changes applied to the linked copy.

To use the Add-on you have to make sure you saved the file you are editing at the moment.

5.3.2 Permanently copy linked objects

Using the Link option has many benefits like keeping your files small and giving a powerful way to work in a large project as a team. However, you must consider the downsides of having most of the assets linked to an external library.

The most troublesome aspect is the fact that you will "lock" the file to your computer. For instance, you won't be able to send the file by email to someone else, because you would need all the corresponding linked libraries. Even a backup could show some problems.

If you lost a folder on your computer with several libraries, all files depending on such assets would open with missing assets. Luckily, we have a simple way to convert any linked object. After the conversion, the file will become part of the file and lose the link to the external library.

How to convert? Go to the **Object → Relations → Make Local** menu and choose what type of data you want to make local (Figure 5.11).

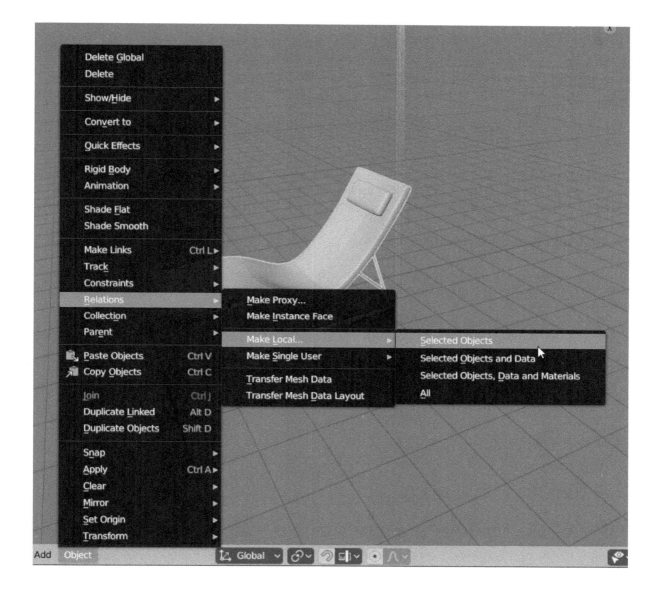

Figure 5.11 - *Make local*

There are multiple options to select, and if you want to get all the information from the file, you must choose the Selected Objects, Data, and Materials. That way, you will have the objects as local data in your project.

5.4 Importing furniture models

Since Blender can import several types of files, we can get a wide range of options regarding assets to use in an architectural project. That will enable you to use libraries with a file like FBX and OBJ, which are quite common online.

Most of those files doesn't require any conversion and will work straight away in Blender. You have to get the file and import it to Blender.

You have to be cautious about file size and polygon count of those files because they can add a significant computational load to your projects. For instance, a simple furniture model in OBJ could easily add a couple of million polygons to a scene.

5.4.1 Clean up and fix furniture assets

One of the downsides of importing external furniture models or assets to Blender is the fact that you will most likely have to perform some cleanup to the model. That is because of differences regarding coordinates and also scale.

You don't have any idea if the author of such model used any scale in the project, which could generate massive objects in your scene.

For instance, we can use as an example of an OBJ file with a furniture model to import. After importing the model, we will check for three potential aspects that could require you to take action:

- Scale and orientation

- Origin point

- Duplicate meshes

In Figure 5.12, you can see the results of an import action with a furniture model from an OBJ file.

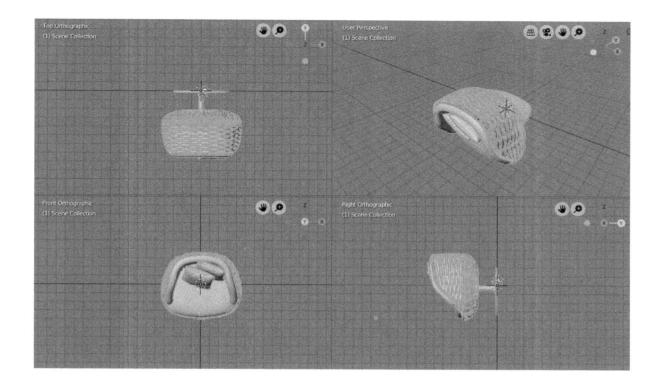

Figure 5.12 - Imported furniture

As you can see from the image, both scale and orientation need a fix. We have to rotate the model -90 degrees in the X-axis and apply a scale of 0.01.

1. Press the R key followed by the S key

2. Type -90

3. Press Return to confirm

4. Press the S key

5. Type 0.02

6. Press Return to confirm

The action will fix both rotation and scale for this model. However, our origin point is not at an optimal location. To make your life easier, you should place the origin point at the bottom center of your model.

You can move the origin point using the 3D Cursor and the Snap tool. With the model selected, go to Edit Mode. Set the selection mode to vertex and with the B key select all vertices from the bottom of your furniture (Figure 5.13).

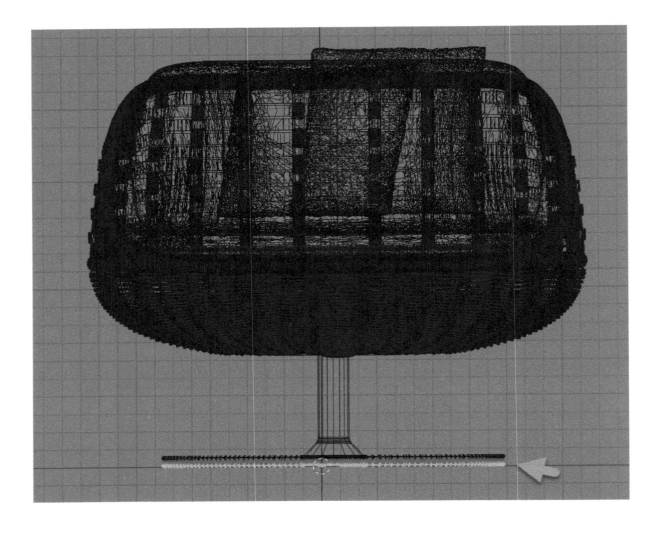

Figure 5.13 - Selected vertices

With the vertices selected:

1. Press the SHIFT+S key
2. Choose the Cursor to selected
3. Go back to Object Mode
4. Open the **Object → Set Origin → Origin to 3D Cursor** menu

That will make your origin point to stay at the bottom of your model not only in the bottom but also at the center of your 3d model.

The last step to ensure you have an optimized model is you check for duplicated meshes. Select the model and go to Edit Mode. Select all vertices with the A key and open the Context Menu with a right-click.

At the menu, you must go to the **Merge Vertices** → **By Distance** option to remove any duplicates. Blender will show the results in the status bar at the bottom of your interface (Figure 5.14).

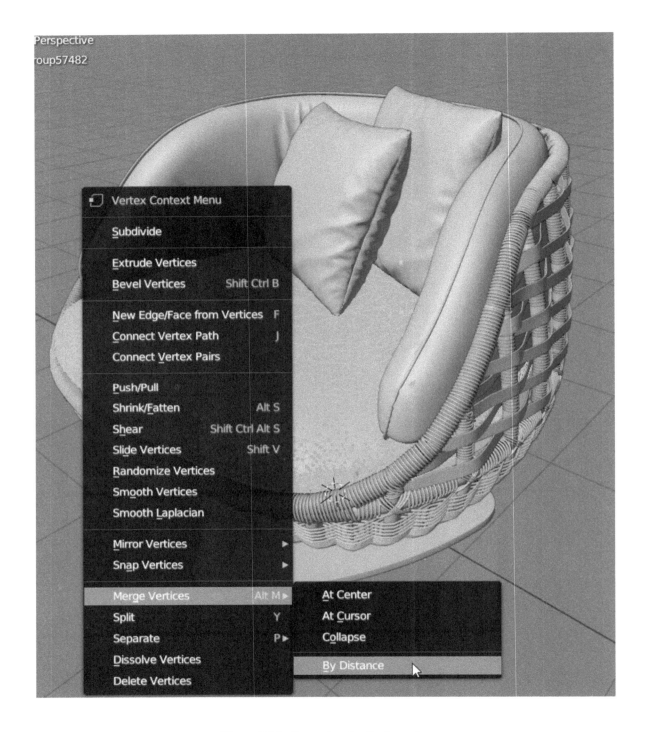

Figure 5.14 - *Removing duplicate meshes*

The check for duplicated meshes is to make sure the author of that model didn't leave any unnecessary geometry behind.

5.5 Prepare models for reuse

What if you have worked on a file and want to prepare it for reuse later? In that case, you may want to take a few precautions to ensure you will quickly be able to get the data and use straight away in Blender.

The first and more obvious step you have to take is to assign meaningful names to any object you want to use in a future project. The reason for that is simple has a direct relation to the Append or Link selection. If you keep using default names, it will be a nightmare to find what you need in a large file.

To assign a name, you have to select the object and go to the Object tab in the Properties editor. Locate the object name field and set the name you want (Figure 5.15). You can also select the object and press F2.

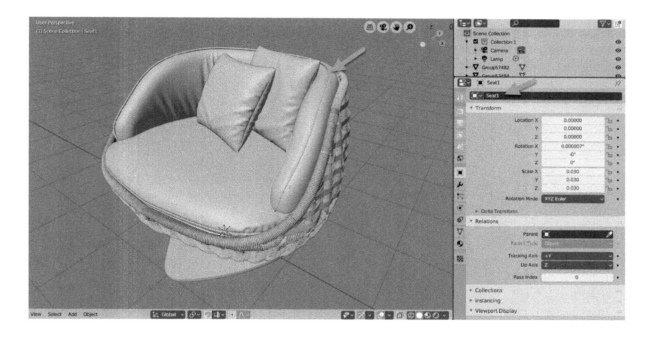

Figure 5.15 - Object name

A few objects have multiple parts, like a dining room set that has a table and several chairs. If you want to make it easy to transfer that data to other files, you could use a collection in Blender.

Select all object you want to use as a group and press the M key. Choose the "New Collection" option. That will add all selected objects to a new collection. Give the collection a name that will help you identify the asset (Figure 5.16).

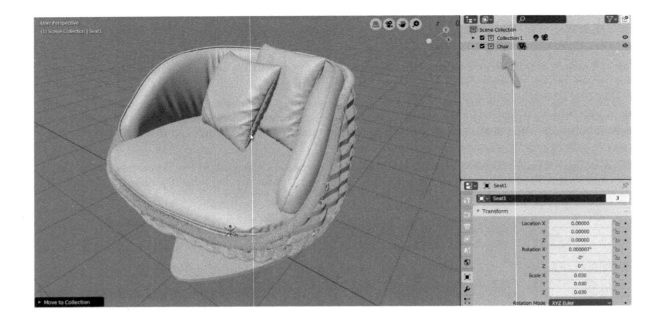

Figure 5.16 - Collection names

A significant advantage of using collections is the fact that you can get multiple objects in the Append and Link selection, and transfer all the objects at once. You have to look for the collection name in the folder called Collection at the file selection.

The last thing you should do to ensure you won't have to make a lot of changes to a 3D model is set the origin point to the bottom of your model. That will be the insertion point for the object after you use the Append or Link tools.

You can easily set the origin point with the 3D Cursor. If you don't remember, go back to the topic *"5.4.1 Cleanup and fix furniture assets"* where we explained how to change the origin point of your assets.

Finally, make a folder in your computer that will store all files with potential assets for reuse. That will be much better than having to search for multiple project locations to get a simple furniture asset.

Tip: As a way to keep your library available in multiple locations, you can use cloud service to keep your Blender files synced with various devices. That way you can always have assets like furniture models, textures, and more continuously available and updated.

What is next?

The next step in an architectural project after you have all the models ready is to start working with the rendering of your 3D models and scene. Regarding rendering, we will discuss a lot of aspects of Cycles and Eevee in the next chapters.

Starting with materials and shaders for architecture in the following chapter, you will learn how to assign and control materials for architectural models. Both Eevee and Cycles supports a wide range of options for textures and even realistic materials in PBR format.

You will learn how to apply and setup materials and textures in the next chapter.

Chapter 6 - Materials and textures for architecture

A unique visualization project will feature not only great lighting but also materials to add context to surfaces. You can create a wide range of effects and materials with Blender.

Unlike many artists might think you can create a single material in Blender and use it to render with both Eevee and Cycles. That is a great benefit and a time saver.

Another great feature of materials that you will learn to use and could make a massive difference in architecture is the use of PBR materials. The collection of textures based on real surfaces that can add an incredible level of realism for any project.

Here is a list of what you will learn:

– How to add materials to objects

– Using shaders to change materials

– Use Nodes in the Shader Editor

– Apply glossy effects for shaders

– Use PBR materials for architecture

– Make architectural glass

– Handling external texture files

6.1 Adding materials to objects

A critical component of any project dealing with architectural visualization is the ability to represent surfaces visually. For that purpose, you will find materials and textures as the best option for the task. They will offer a quick and straightforward way to assigning effects like transparency, reflections, and texture display on surfaces.

In Blender, you will find support to use several types of textures and materials. Those materials will work on both Cycles or Eevee, and in most cases, you will have to make small tweaks in settings to use them on projects with both renderers.

How to apply materials to objects in Blender?

Before we deal with details related to the material, it is important to list a few facts regarding materials:

– Materials exist in Blender as an independent data type. You will associate them to an object, but you can have multiple objects sharing the same material

154

- If a material doesn't have any object associated, Blender will erase the material the next time you save and close the file

- Materials can have one of the multiple shaders for surface composition

- A shader will set up how the material reflects light

- Materials can use Nodes to allow more complex and sophisticated setups. To use Nodes, we have the Shader Editor

- Each material must have a unique name and assigning meaningful names is vital for both reuse and project organization

How to assign materials to any object in Blender?

To add and edit aspects of materials in Blender, we will use the Materials tab in the Properties Editor (Figure 6.1).

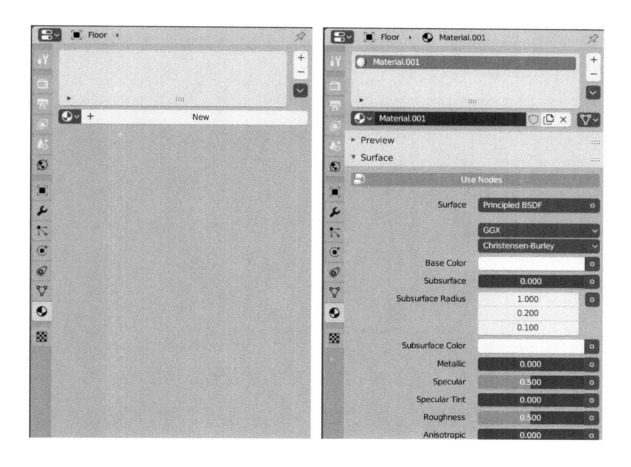

Figure 6.1 - *Materials Editor*

There you will see all the options related to materials and textures. If an object doesn't have any materials, you will see a button with an option to add a new material, or a list to edit options for the assigned material (Figure 6.2).

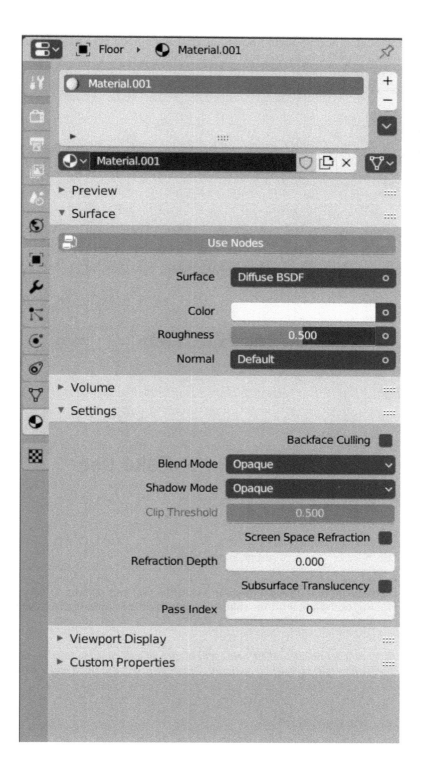

Figure 6.2 - Editing material

At the top of the material editor, you will find all the controls related to managing materials and objects. In Figure 6.3, you have a list of the main controls for materials.

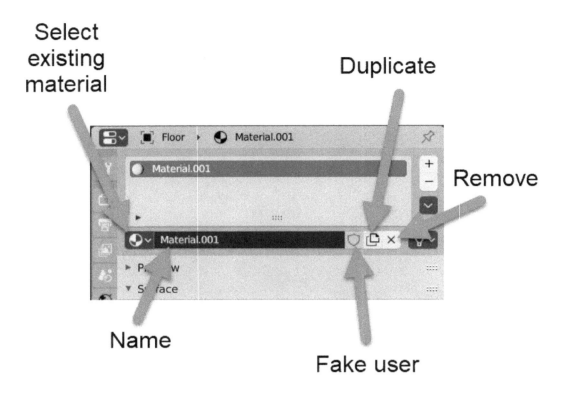

Figure 6.3 - *Material controls*

If you want to use a material that already exists in your file, you can use the selector to expand a list of available materials. Having materials with meaningful names will be a great help to select the surface you need quickly.

Info: Any material that has a zero next to their name will be part of a data purge from Blender the next time you close the file. That means Blender will exclude the material. To prevent that you must add a Fake User to the material.

6.1.1 Using shaders for materials

One of the critical components of any material is the shader selection for each material that will set the behavior of a surface regarding light. There are several types of shaders available in Blender. If you click on the selector at the top of your material editor, you will see the list of available shaders (Figure 6.4).

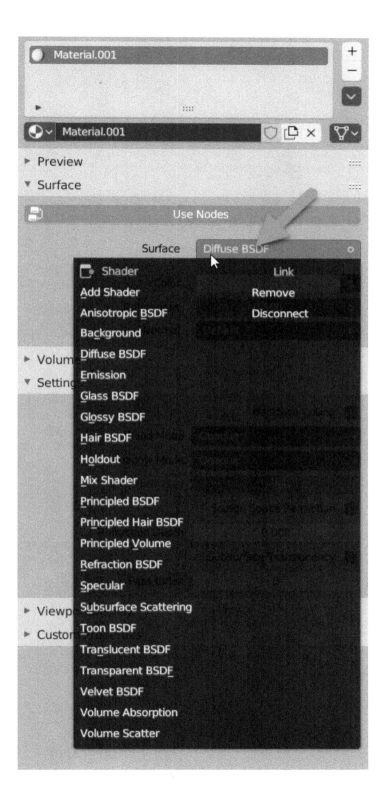

159

Figure 6.4 - *List of shaders*

Here is a brief description of what you can do with the essential shaders:

- **Diffuse BSDF**: Used to get simple colors for materials with a no reflective surface

- **Glossy BSDF**: If you need a reflective surface you should use this shader

- **Glass BSDF**: A surface prepared to represent the visual aspect of glass using advanced effects

- **Principled BSDF**: A powerful and multipurpose shader that can receive PBR textures

- **Mix Shader**: In some case, you will have to blend multiple shaders to get an effect. Using this shader will allow you to connect and mix multiple shaders

For instance, if you select the Diffuse BSDF, you will have only a selector to get a color. That is one of the most straightforward types of shaders. If you only need a surface that represents a dull color, you can use this shader.

The Material Editor will even give you a preview window that shows the result of your material setup without the need to render.

Info: The BSDF next to each shader name means Bidirectional Scattering Distribution Function.

You can select any shader in the Material Editor to use with an object, which will have the options regarding that shader displayed below the selector. The options at the Material Editor will allow you to have a wide range of materials ready for any project. However, to use all the power of your materials, we must move to the Shader Editor.

6.2 Using the Shader Editor

The Shader Editor is a powerful tool in Blender to craft materials and other aspects of a scene using something called Nodes. With the Nodes, you have a visual tool to build materials in a similar way of a workflow. You will connect Nodes to get the desired effect.

Once you open the Shader Editor, you will be able to add new Nodes using the SHIFT+A keys or the Add menu. The editor is available from the editor selector or multiple WorkSpaces like the Rendering → Shading.

A few things regarding Nodes and the Shader Editor:

- If you select an object and no Nodes appear, you probably must press the "Use Nodes" button in the Material Editor

- All keys used for modeling in Blender works the same way in the Shader Editor for selection and Node manipulation

- Each Node might have input, output sockets, or both of them

- To connect Nodes, you will click and drag from an output socket (right side) to an input socket (left side)

- Use the color codes from each socket to find what data type they carry. For instance, you will see yellow circles representing color data

- Each material can have dozens of Nodes depending on the material you are trying to make

- You can break the connection between Nodes by holding down the CTRL key and clicking and dragging the right mouse button. That will turn the mouse into a "knife" that can cut the connection lines

A simple way to demonstrate how to use the Nodes is with image texture. We can make a material that has a texture as the primary color for the Diffuse BSDF shader.

The first thing you will need is a material using the Diffuse BSDF as the main shader. If you have a material like this one and open the Shader Editor, you will see the Nodes representing this setup (Figure 6.5).

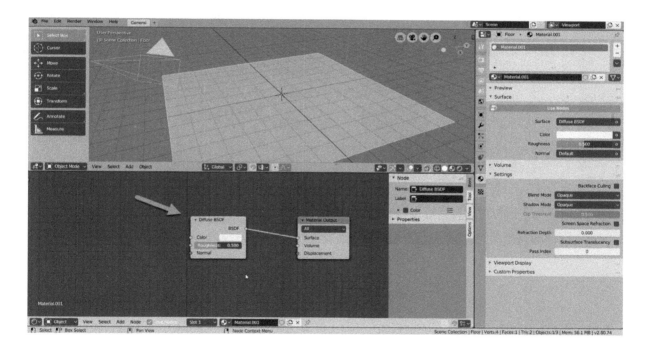

Figure 6.5 - *Shader Editor with material*

Press the SHIFT+A key and go to Texture → Image Texture to add a new Node that supports external image files. At the Node, you should press the Open button and locate a texture file.

After opening the image file, you can click and drag from the output socket from your Image Texture Node to the input socket of the Diffuse BSDF (Figure 6.6).

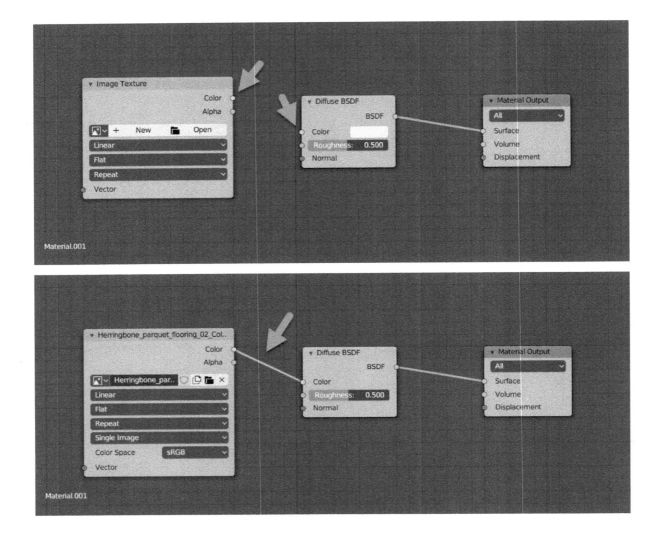

Figure 6.6 - *Connecting two Nodes*

In the preview area of your Material Editor, you will be able to see the texture used to represent the color of your material.

Info: External textures works similarly than furniture files using the Link option. Use the same tools and options to manage this resource.

162

6.3 Glossy materials for architecture

The Diffuse BSDF is a simple shader that can make surfaces with a solid color that won't have any other effect regrind light reflection. But, in most of the surfaces you will work in architecture, we have some level of reflection for lights.

You can make reflective surfaces using the Glossy BSDF shader or a combination of a Glossy BSDF and Diffuse BSDF. If you apply the glossy shader directly to a surface and render the results, you will get a reflection effect (Figure 6.7).

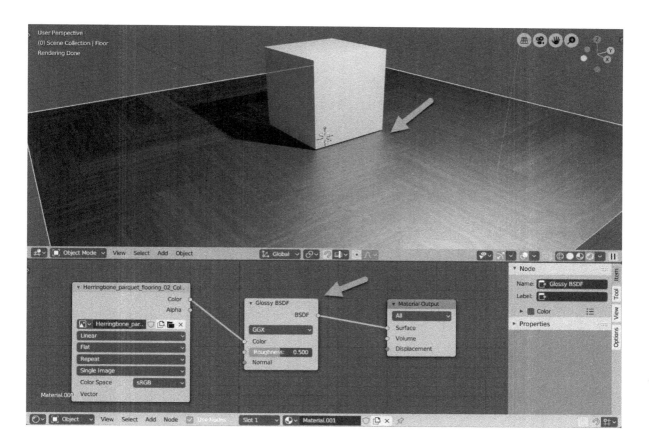

Figure 6.7 - Glossy material

With the Roughness option from the Glossy BSDF, you can control the level of blurriness for the reflection. Lower values will result in more blur.

Another option to use the Glossy BSDF is to mix it with the Diffuse BSDF. For instance, we can get a material that has an Image Texture connected to the Diffuse BSDF and apply a glossy effect. To do that you will need a Mix Shader Node.

Press the SHIFT+A keys in the Shader Editor and add from the **Shader → Mix Shader**. The Mix Shader allows us to blend two shaders by connecting each one of them to their input sockets (Figure 6.8).

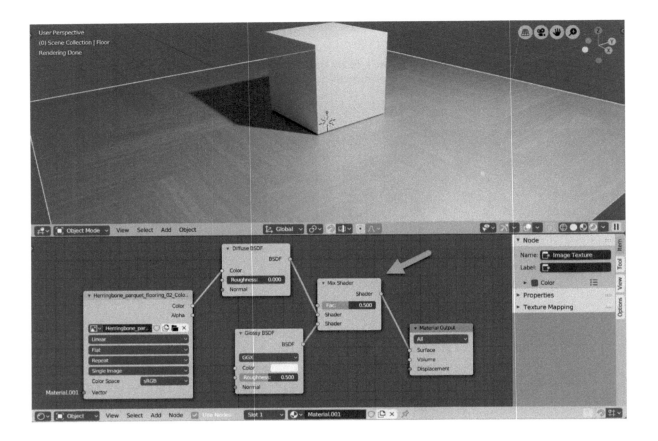

Figure 6.8 - Mixing two shaders

You can also stack multiple Mix Shaders to blend more than two shaders.

The result for a material that has an Image Texture with the Glossy BSDF is a blurred reflection that you could easily use for a floor in interior projects (Figure 6.9).

164

Figure 6.9 - *Blurred reflections with texture*

The Glossy BSDF could also receive the Image Texture directly since it has an input socket for color data.

6.4 Physically-based render materials

One of the most powerful ways of adding materials to any architectural visualization project in Blender is with the use of PBR materials. The acronym PBR means *Physically Based Render* and classifies a group of textures prepared to make realistic surfaces.

A typical PBR material will feature several maps of textures that you should use in multiple channels to make a realistic surface. For instance, you will get a map for:

- Diffuse

- Roughness

- Normal

- Ambient Occlusion

- Displacement

Instead of using multiple shaders to blend all this information, we can use the Principled BSDF from the shader list of Blender. The shader is a powerful collection of options to craft multiple types of materials. If you decide to only use PBR materials for your projects, you can easily ignore all other types of shaders.

Before we start to use and setup materials using the Principled BSDF, we have to get some of those assets. Nowadays, you will find several free sources of PBR materials online, which offers textures with a public domain license. Here are a few of those libraries:

– CC0Textures → https://cc0textures.com

– CGBookcase → https://www.cgbookcase.com

– TextureHaven → https://texturehaven.com

Some of their materials will feature textures up to 4K resolution (4096 x 4096) pixels.

6.4.1 Using the Principled BSDF

The first thing you need to use a shader like the Principled BSDF to make PBR materials is pack with all the necessary maps. We will use for the following example, a material called Wood that features multiple maps for a PBR surface.

A PBR material will usually come as a ZIP file that you must extract to use all the maps in Blender. Inside our material, you will see five different maps:

– Color

– Roughness

– Ambient Occlusion

– Normal

– Displacement

From this list, we can start choosing between the normal and displacement maps. They both have e similar goal, which is to add details to the surface like grooves, bumps, and scratches.

With the normal map, we can apply the effect to any surfaces, regardless of the geometry. The displacement will require you to have a high-density mesh to get the best effect. In our example, we can pick the normal map to add such details to the material.

That leaves us with four maps to use in the Shader Editor. Add material to an object and select the Principled BSDF as the main shader. Go to the Shader Editor and add four Image Texture Nodes (Figure 6.10).

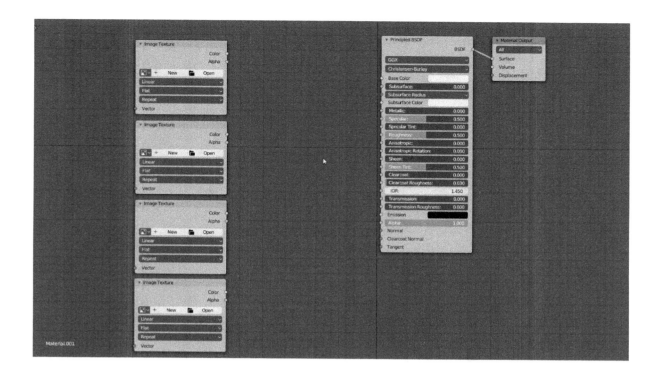

Figure 6.10 - *Image Texture Nodes*

You can add just one and using the SHIFT+D keys duplicate the Nodes.

Tip: You can also drag and drop the image files from your file manager to the Shader Editor window in Blender. They will receive an Image Texture Node automatically.

Using the Open button, you can select each of the texture files from our PBR material. In the Nodes containing both the Roughness and Normal maps, you should change the Color Space to No-Data (Figure 6.11).

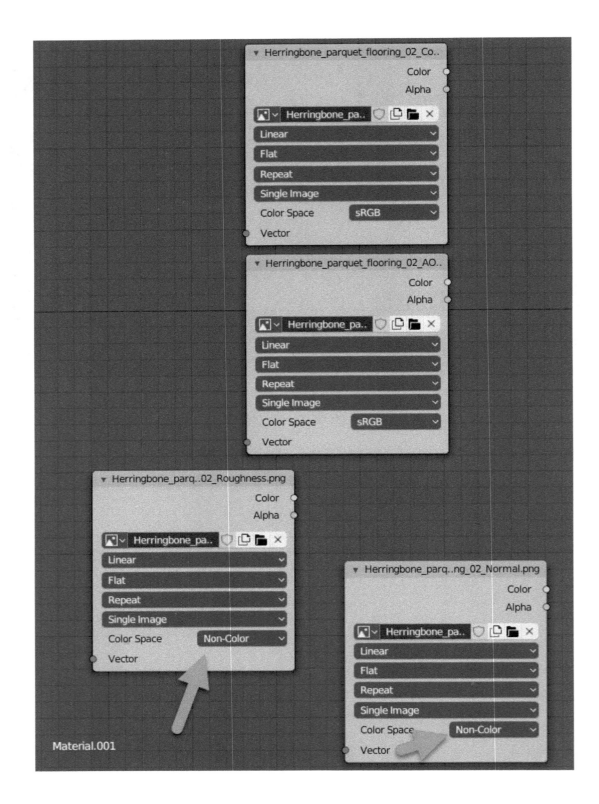

Figure 6.11 - *Color Space*

The change is necessary because those textures don't affect the color of our material.

Now that we have all the Image Texture Nodes ready, we can start adding connections. You can begin with the texture representing the roughness map. Connect that Node to the input socket for the Roughness in the Principled BSDF.

For the Normal map, we need an additional Node to transform the texture in normal map data. Press the SHIFT+A keys and add from the **Vector → Normal Map** a new Node. Connect the normal map to the Normal Map Node. From the Normal Map Node, you can finally connect to the Principled BSDF input socket for the Normal (Figure 6.12).

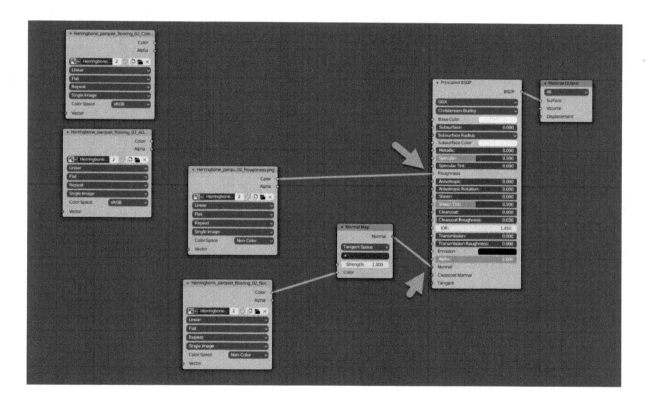

Figure 6.12 - *Normal and Roughness*

Both input sockets will use the data from our image textures, and you don't have to make any adjustments regarding values.

The next step is to add the color and ambient occlusion maps. If you didn't have the ambient occlusion, we could connect the color directly to the Base Color input socket.

Since the ambient occlusion will also deal with color, which generates an effect called contact shadows or proximity shadows, we must mix them before connecting to the Base Color.

Press the SHIFT+A key and add a Node from **Color → MixRGB**. Connect both the color and ambient occlusion to the MixRGB and connect the output of this Node to the Base Color input socket.

In the end, you will have the setup shown in Figure 6.13 for the PBR material.

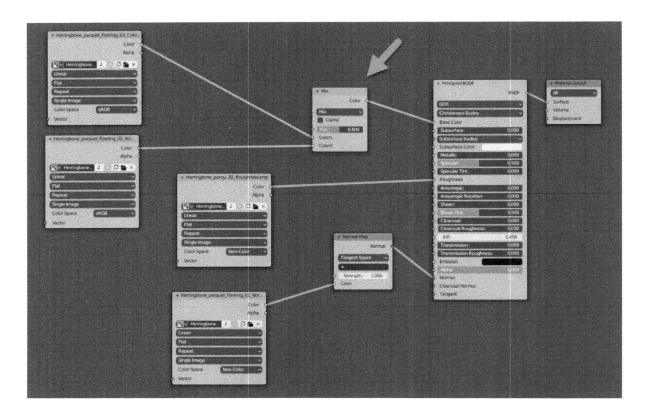

Figure 6.13 - *PBR material*

You can use this PBR material as a template for all other types of materials you have to use in Blender. They work with both Cycles and Eevee and will usually feature the same types of maps.

6.5 Texture tiling for architecture

Even with PBR materials working as a powerful way to add advanced materials to surfaces, you will probably need some level control over tilling. What is the tilling effect? Some texture will cover a small area in your 3D model, and you might need to set the texture size.

170

For instance, in a model that has a parquet wood floor texture, you could have large blocks of parquet that you must scale down. With the tiling controls, you can set the number of repetitions Blender will use to cover a large area.

Tip: To use a tilling effect with textures, you must ensure the texture is seamless. When you tile a seamless texture, they won't have any visible borders.

To control the tilling effect for textures and PBR materials, we will need two additional Nodes:

– Add the Input → Texture Coordinate

– Add the Vector → Mapping

Those two Nodes will help you control the tilling effect. You will connect the Generated output socket to the Mapping. From the Mapping, you should make connections to all your Image Texture Nodes (Figure 6.14).

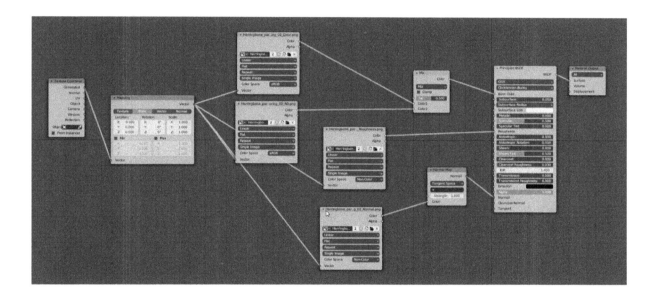

Figure 6.14 *- Tilling setup*

Notice that you have a field in the Mapping called Scale. There you can control the size Blender will use for each texture. If you increase the scale for all axis, you will reduce the size of your images.

Having a lower value will generate the opposite effect (Figure 6.15).

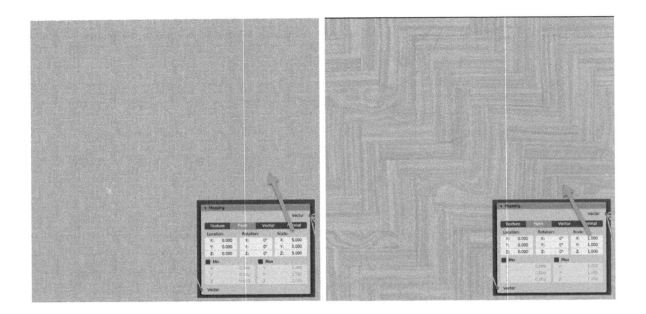

Figure 6.15 - *Tilling control with scale*

Keep in mind that some textures will have areas in the image that will appear in a repeated way.

Tip: For better performance and tilling effects, you should prefer textures with square size. Besides the square size, they also must use dimensions in a power of two. For instance, a commonly used texture size would be 128 x 128, 256 x 256, 512 x 512, 1024 x 1024, 2048 x 2048, and 4096 x 4096.

6.6 Transparent materials for architecture

To create transparent materials, you have two shaders that will help to make those types of surfaces quickly, which are the Glass BSDF and the Transparent BSDF.

For the cases where you need simple transparency with no reflections, you can use straight away the Transparent BSDF. It will give you a simple transparency effect. For a more sophisticated result, you will apply the Glass BSDF material to the surface (Figure 6.16).

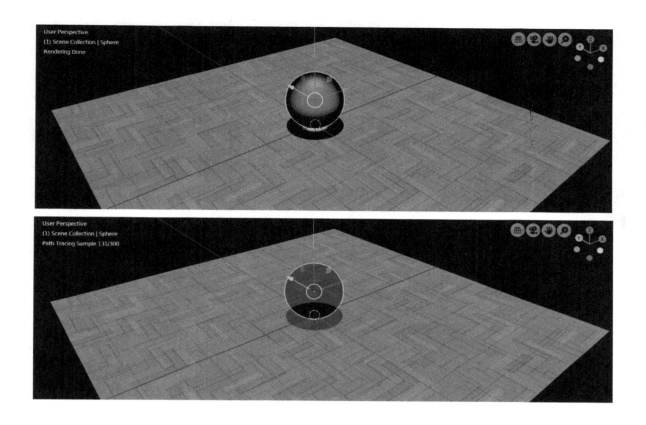

Figure 6.16 - *Comparing the Transparent and Glass*

In the Glass BSDF (top), you will find the same type of control from the Glossy BSDF shader, which will allow you to add blurred reflections with the roughness.

6.7 Architectural glass in Blender

Even with the possibility of working with transparent materials, you will find that such shader alone won't give optimal results for architecture. Because, if you try to use the material in a glass panel for either interiors or exteriors, the material will block light.

In Figure 6.17, you can see the results of a Glass BSDF material applied to a window.

Figure 6.17 - *Glass material*

What we need is the glass panel to let the light go through the material, and still, behave like glass with reflections and more — something like Image 6.18 shows.

Figure 6.18 - Architectural glass

How to make that setup? To make architectural glass, we have to add some more Nodes:

– Input → Light Path

– Converter → Add (2x)

– Shader → Transparent BSDF

– Shader → Mix Shader

With those Nodes, we can make an architectural glass. The process requires you to:

1. From the Light Path, connect the Is Shadow Ray and Is Diffuse Ray to the Math Node

2. Connect that same Math Node to the Second Math Node

3. To the remaining input socket of the second Math Node, connect the Is Glossy Ray of your Light Path

In Figure 6.19, you can see the results of the process.

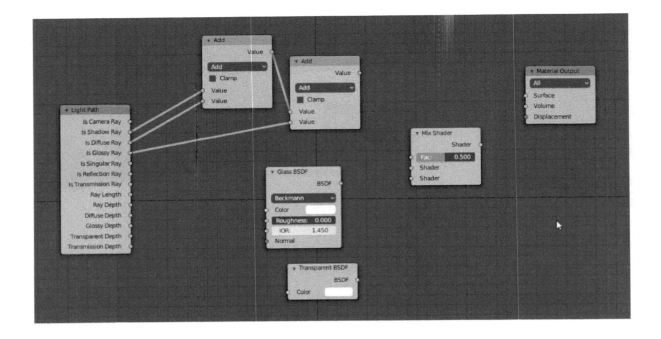

Figure 6.19 - *Connecting the first Nodes*

Now, from the last Math Node, connect it to the Fac of your Mix Shader.

Connect to the Mix Shader input socket both your Glass BSDF and Transparent BSDF. The final result for the architectural glass material should be like Figure 6.20.

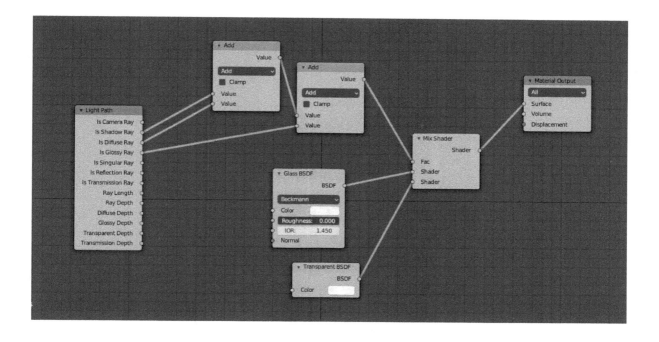

Figure 6.20 - *Architectural glass Nodes*

If you apply that material to any panel that should look like glass, it will reflect the surroundings and let the light go through. Unfortunately, you will see the effect only in Cycles and not in Eevee.

6.8 Embedding textures to Blender files

When you open any image texture file in Blender, it will become part of the data assets listed inside the project file. That means you can select each and any one of the files used in a project, whenever you have to open texture files again (Figure 6.21).

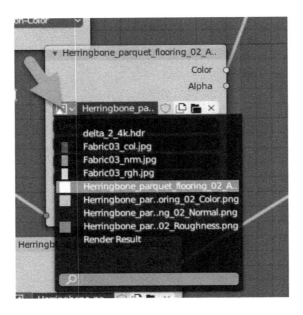

Figure 6.21 - Texture files in project

You have to click on the selector right next to any Node requiring images.

Even with the images being part of that internal list, they are still external resources. That means if you have to move, copy, or transfer the project file, you will also need to copy every single texture file. If you open a file in Blender and see a magenta background or surface, it means Blender could not find a texture file.

Regarding texture files, you have two options to fix that you can enable the pack option for external data. In the File menu, you will find an option called External Data. There you will see a list with options related to external assets (Figure 6.22).

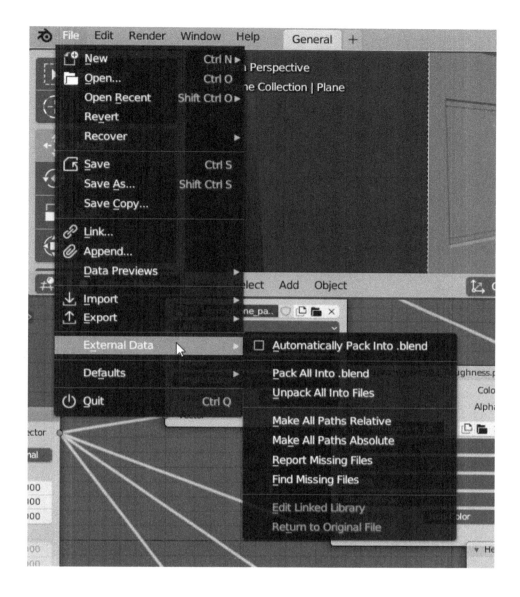

Figure 6.22 - External assets

If you enable the "Automatically Pack Into .blend" option, you will embed all texture files to the project. That will make your life easier by attaching all textures for materials to your project.

You have to be cautious about:

- **Filesize increase**: Your file will now have the 3D data and also all the images

- **Texture edit**: To edit a texture you will have to Unpack the file to access an image

As a good practice for textures and avoid problems with the unpack of data you should always put the texture files for a project in the same folder, or a subfolder of your main project file in Blender. That will generate relative paths to the texture files.

After you unpack any image files, Blender will try to write the file to disk using the same structure you used when embedding the material.

Whats is next?

The materials are just part of the equation that will guide you to a great architectural visualization with Blender. You will also have to choose the render engine you would like to use for the project.

In the following two chapters, you will learn how to use and prepare a render for architecture using wither Cycles or Eevee. The traditional approach of Cycles will give you more realism at the cost of render time. On the other hand, you have realtime render with Eevee that will give away some realism for instantaneous renders.

Chapter 7 - Real-time rendering with Eevee

From all the new features of Blender 2.8, a significant number of artists will state that Eevee is among the best. What is Eevee? That is a real-time render engine that is revolutionary for Blender and puts it side by side with the most advanced technologies for architectural visualization.

You will be able to get impressive visuals for projects with renders taking just a few seconds.

Unlike Cycles that uses Path Tracing, you will get Eevee using a technique called Rasterization via OpenGL 3.3. That is the same method you will find in 3D Game Engines. The tradeoff of this technology is realism. It won't be able to deliver the same visuals from Cycles, but it will get close enough for a lot of projects.

Here is what you will learn about Eevee:

– Starting a render with Eevee

– Settings aspects of the render like sampling

– Baking indirect lights

– Control shadow quality

– Prepare a scene with Sunlight

– Use Environment Textures

– Setting cameras for architecture

7.1 Rendering with Eevee

It is time to start rendering our projects using one of the most recent additions to Blender, which is the real-time render engine called Eevee. To use Eevee and select it as the primary renderer, you don't have to do anything. That is because Blender will choose Eevee as the default render.

Where can you find the renderer list in Blender? If you go to the Properties Editor, you will see the renderer list at the Render tab. There you will be able to select different render engines and also choose options regarding the active render (Figure 7.1).

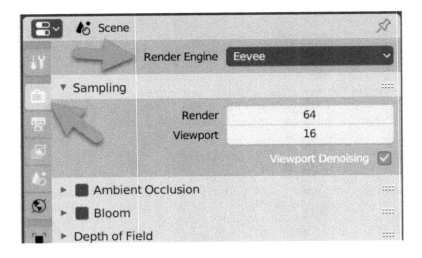

Figure 7.1 - *Renderer selection*

Another tab from the Properties Editor that you should also take a close look is the Output. There you will find all options regarding how you will render the images in Blender (Figure 7.2).

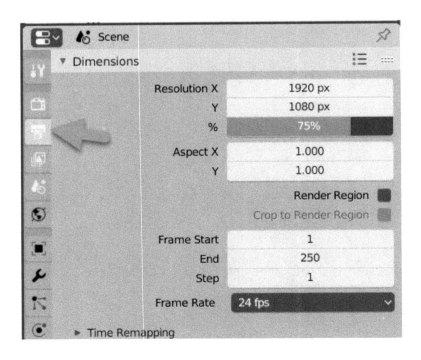

Figure 7.2 - *Render output*

For instance, at the top, you will have the resolution to set how big your images will be in pixels. Below the resolution options, you will even be able to use a scale factor to make quick changes to the size. A common practice is to make test renders with a smaller size to speed up the output.

Since Eevee can render the images in real-time, the option will become more useful for Cycles.

At the Output field you can change the file format you will use to save your renders. If you want to keep maximum quality, you should save the renders in PNG first and later convert them to a smaller format like JPG.

Since Eevee can work in real-time, you can use the rendered shading mode and do all the work viewing the project as a render. The shortcut for the shading modes is the Z key.

7.2 Render checklist with Eevee

Similarly to Cycles, you will find that Eevee will use a standard set of options for most scenes. There are a few settings that you should always use with a scene and others that are optional.

Those settings that are optional will depend on several factors based on the current project you are working.

Here is a list of items you should always add to a scene in Eevee:

1. Materials on most surfaces, and if possible use PBR textures

2. Setup an Environment Texture with an HDR map

3. Add one or more Irradiance Volumes to the scene

4. Use a Reflection Cubemap

5. Add a Sun to the scene *(optional)*

6. Add Area Lights to doors, windows, and behind the camera *(optional)*

7. Bake Indirect Lights to the render

8. Adjust the shadow quality in the Render tab

9. Turn on Screen Space Reflections and Ambient Occlusion

10. Evaluate the use of Bloom for your renders

11. Use Color Correction to fine-tune your render illumination and colors

With those steps, you will eventually be able to set up all the scenes you will work in Eevee for architecture. The steps marked as optional will depend on several factors.

For instance, you might use an HDR image for the background that can provide enough light to simulate the Sun, which will make the use of a dedicated light for that purpose unnecessary.

Along with the chapter, you will learn to use each one of those features in the checklist.

7.3 Rendering an interior with Eevee

The best way to learn how to set up a scene in Eevee is with a practical example. In Figure 7.3, you can look at the interior. We will set up with Eevee.

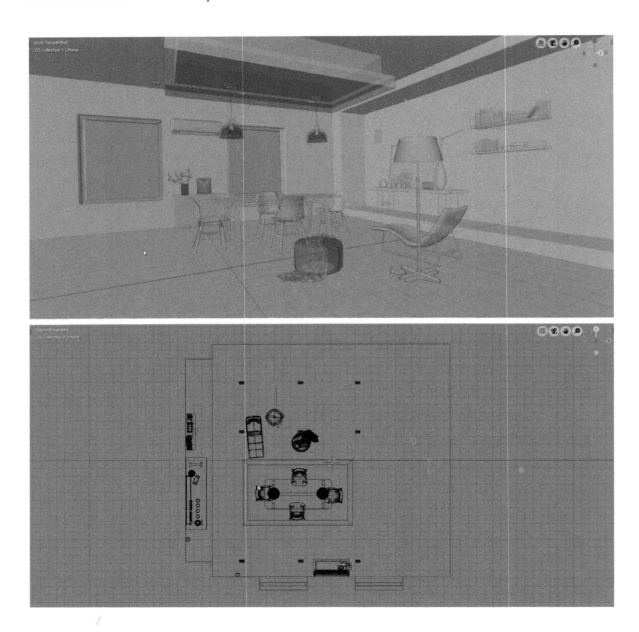

Figure 7.3 - *Interior scene*

You will notice that we have all the furniture and assets in place along with the materials for the scene.

One aspect of your modeling projects that you must take special care is the relations between windows and lights. For each scene, you will have to find a way to make light to get into the room.

You may have a limited area for windows, which may require additional regions. For instance, look at the side of the room. We have an open space that won't be present at the final design of this space but will help with the lighting (Figure 7.4).

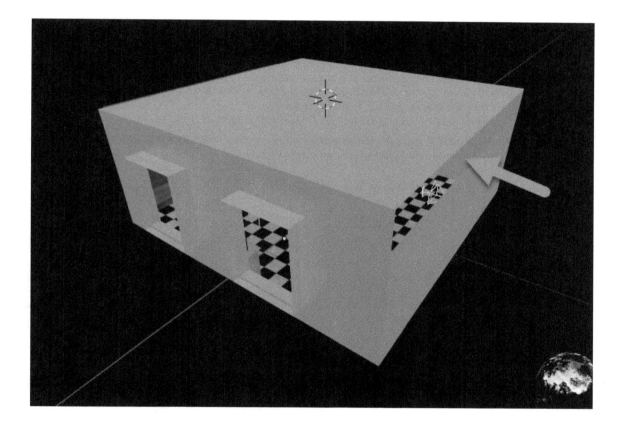

Figure 7.4 - *Open space*

Since it won't appear at the final render, you don't have to worry about that in the design stage. The rule works for most of the features and settings of architectural visualization design.

Use all tools available to make an excellent looking image. Even removing parts of the model to facilitate the render, always making sure it won't appear in the final images.

7.4 Adding an Environment Map

If you start to move the objects around in your scene using the Rendered mode, you will watch shadows and a better overall look at materials, in case you have one applied to the surfaces. But, we still have to add a few elements to the scene that will have a significant impact on the final result.

Using an Environment Map in your scene will have a profound impact on colors and reflections for the scene. That is a rule you should follow with both Eevee and Cycles.

What is the Environment Map? That is a texture you apply to the background of your scene, which might help with illumination and also reflect on glossy surfaces.

The best results for architecture will come from HDR textures that you apply in the background. They will generate natural colors and reflections. How to get this type of surface?

Nowadays, you will find several free online libraries offering HDR maps in the public domain. One of the best sources is HDRHaven (https://hdrihaven.com). There you will find a wide range of HDR maps to download with resolutions going up to 16K (16384 pixels).

Info: Some artists don't use HDR maps for the background. Instead, they choose to use a plain white color. The result will be a constant light from the environment, like an overcast sky.

To demonstrate how to use an HDR map, we will use the HDR map shown in Figure 7.5.

Figure 7.5 - HDR map

A vital feature of an HDR map is the type of light and shadow it will generate. Some HDR maps will create hard edge shadows without the need of Sunlight. Make sure you check the preview before downloading an HDR for your project.

Once you have the HDR map in your computer, we can add that to the scene in Blender. Go to the World tab at the Properties Editor and look for the Surface field if you see a button "Use Nodes" press it to show all options.

At the Color field, you have to press the button on the right, with the small dot at the middle, and from the list of options pick the Environment Texture (Figure 7.6).

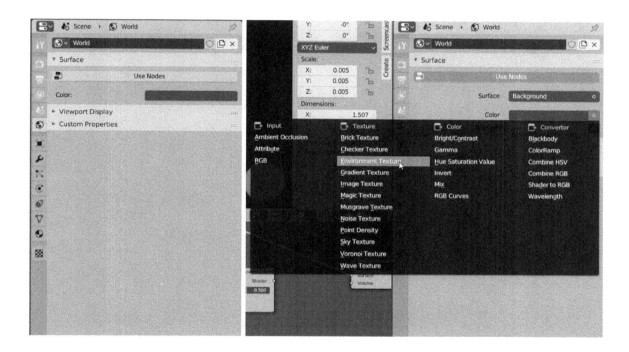

Figure 7.6 - Environment Texture

Use the open button to pick the HDR map from your hard drive and use it as the background for your scene.

7.4.1 How to hide the HDR map in Eevee?

After adding the HDR map to the background, you will notice that you will have the texture appearing in the background. That is normal for an environment map.

In Cycles, we have an easy way of hiding the HDR map to the camera and for render, but in Eevee, we still don't have this option. If you want to hide the texture in Eevee, we have to use a trick by adding an object to cover the HDR map.

The technique consists of using a Sphere and scaling it up until your scene is inside the object. Using the SHIFT+A key add a UV Sphere to the scene and apply a scale with the S key until your entire scene is inside the object (Figure 7.7).

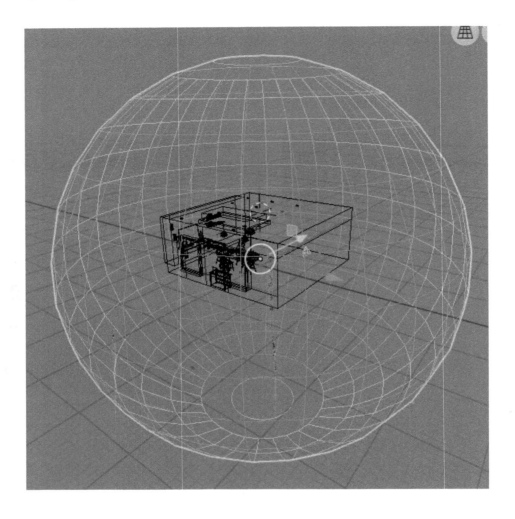

Figure 7.7 - *Scene inside object*

With the sphere still selected you have to:

1. Go to Edit Mode

2. Select all vertices from the sphere

3. Go to the Mesh → Normals → Recalculate outside menu

4. Go to the Face → Shade Smooth menu to finish

By following all these steps, you will have a massive sphere in the background between your model and the HDR map. Why did we have to recalculate the normals? A normal in 3D is the visible side of an object, and by making the visible side of our object pointing to the interior, the outside will become "invisible."

If you try to render the scene now, you won't see the HDR map anymore. But, with the normals pointing to the interior, the lights and reflections still work.

7.5 Using the Irradiance Volume and Cubemap

Even with the use of an HDR map in the background, rendered in Eevee at this point won't be impressive. We are still far away from a realistic result. The main reason for that is because we are still not considering indirect lights from all the sources.

When you decide to use Eevee to render a scene, you must use an object called Irradiance Volume to set an area where Eevee will calculate indirect lights.

To make an Irradiance Volume, you will press the SHIFT+A key and go to the Light Probe → Irradiance Volume (Figure 7.8).

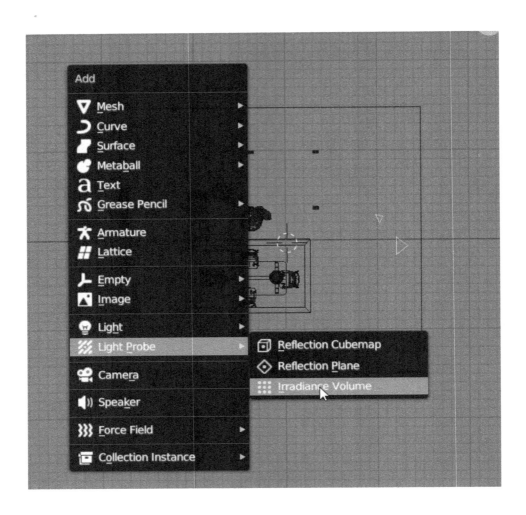

Figure 7.8 - Irradiance Volume

The Irradiance Volume has a cube-like shape with small dots scattered inside. After you add the cache to your scene, the next step is to scale it with the S key until it surrounds the entire 3D model (Figure 7.9).

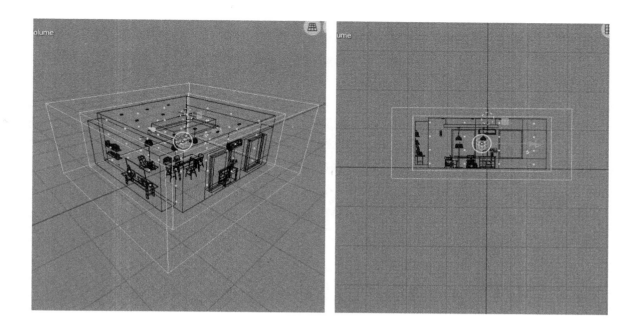

Figure 7.9 - *Scaling the Irradiance Volume*

If any part of the model stays outside the Irradiance Volume it won't be part of the indirect light calculation, and therefore have a much lower light quality. In some cases, you can even use multiple caches if the shape of your project is irregular as long as you have everything inside the cache volume.

You can control the number of dots in the interior of your cache using the Object Data tab in the Properties Editor. Just select the cache and open that tab. For most projects, the default value of four dots, or samples, will give excellent results (Figure 7.10).

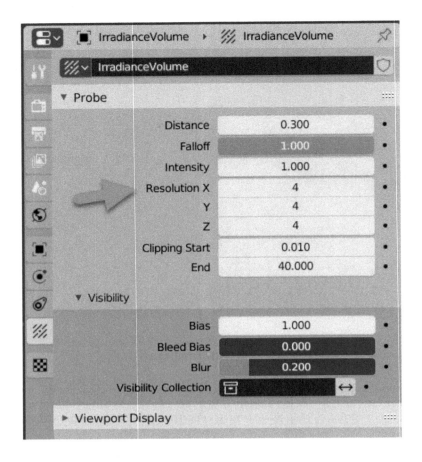

Figure 7.10 - *Volume resolution*

At the 3D Viewport, you might see some improved lights just by adding the Irradiance Volume. But, we still need an extra element to complete the setup for a scene with Eevee. We need a Reflection Cubemap to add a glossy effect to the scene materials.

What is a Reflection Cubemap? Since Eevee can't process reflections from objects based on materials, we need a helper object that will provide all the calculations for reflections. That will be the Cubemap.

Press the SHIFT+A keys, and from the Light Probe group add a Reflection Cubemap (Figure 7.11).

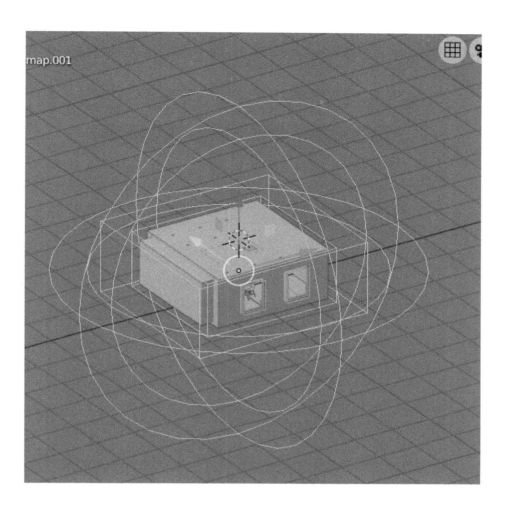

Figure 7.11 - *Adding a Cubemap*

Select the Cubemap and with the S key scale it up until the whole scene is inside the probe shape.

7.6 Adding lights to the scene

For this particular scene, we could use alongside the HDR map in the background some additional light sources. The main objective for this project is to get an overcast look, which will give a more constant type of light.

You could use a Sun and also Area Lights. It is typical for architectural projects using either Eevee or Cycles to use those lights.

In our case, we will use only Area Lights to add more energy coming from windows. Besides the windows, we will also place an additional light behind the camera.

Using the SHIFT+A keys add one Area Light to the scene and adjust the scale of the light to fit a window space. You can change the light settings and make it use a rectangular shape (Figure 7.12).

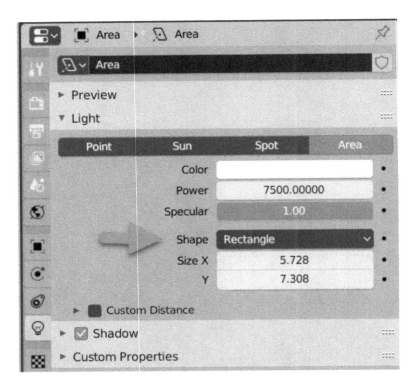

Figure 7.12 - Light settings

Duplicate the light to make it fit the other window. And make another copy that should fit the large window on the back of the camera (Figure 7.13).

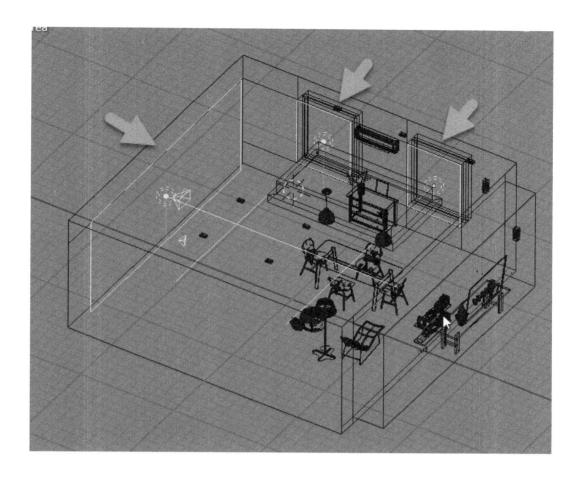

Figure 7.13 - *Area lights locations*

If you don't want shadows from those lights, you can disable the shadow option.

Later you should make tests with the Power settings of each light to evaluate how strong they are for the scene.

Tip: Use the Rendered mode to evaluate the results of your scene and make adjustments to the lights.

7.7 Baking Indirect Lights

The scene already has an Irradiance Volume and a Reflection Cubemap that will add more realism to the project. We can now start to bake the indirect lights of the scene to the surfaces.

Go to the Render tab, and you will find in the Eevee options all settings for the Indirect Lights (Figure 7.14).

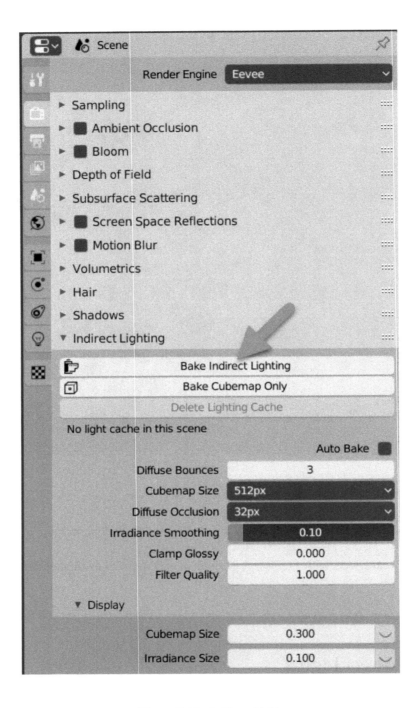

Figure 7.14 - Indirect Lights

There you will see an option called "Bake Indirect Lights" to start calculating the results of our scene. If you press this button, the scene will have all indirect lights recorded to the surfaces. You will see a progress bar at the bottom of your interface showing the calculation progress (Figure 7.15).

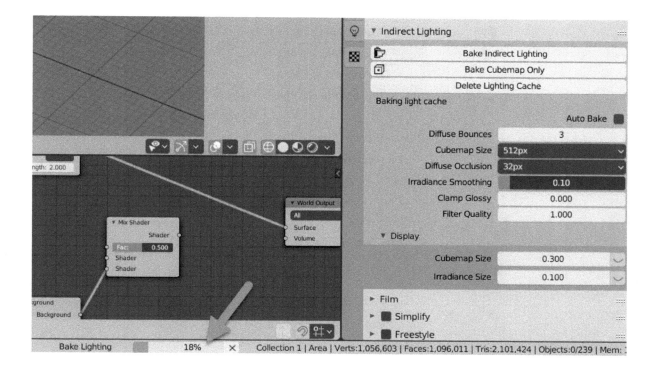

Figure 7.15 - Calculation progress

Depending on the scene size and complexity, it may take a few seconds to process.

After you have the cache for the indirect lights, Blender will display how big they are at the same menu (Figure 7.16).

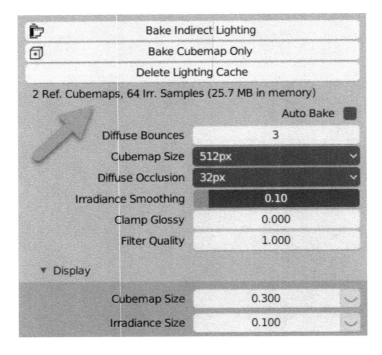

Figure 7.16 - Indirect Lights baking

At the bottom of this panel, you will see some information regarding the light baking. For instance, you can see how big the bake is and the number of probes it is using.

If you want to make adjustments to the lights, you can delete the solution using the "Delete Lighting Cache" button.

A few things you can do to improve your indirect lights:

– **Increase the Diffuse Bounces**: The default value is 3, and that controls the number of bounces the light will perform on surfaces. Using a value of 4 will already improve the lights

– **Cubemap Size**: Increase the size of your Cubemap from 512px to 1024px or more. That will result in better reflections at the cost of longer processing times for baking.

– **Clamp glossy**: Using glossy surfaces may result in noise for rendering. Increase the default value of zero to add a "filter" to remove some of that noise.

Every time you make changes to the indirect lights settings, you will have to process the baking again. You can enable the "Auto Bake" to make Blender process any changes to probes automatically.

7.7.1 Sampling with Eevee

At this point, you will start to see some noise in the render of any scene with Eevee. If you decide to use glossy materials, the noise will become even more evident. What controls the amount of processing you will have at the 3D Viewport is the Sampling (Figure 7.17).

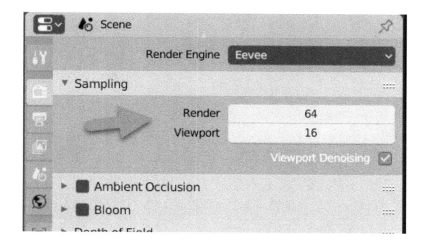

Figure 7.17 - *Sampling for Eevee*

The number of samples will set the interactions used to calculate lights in real-time. With higher values, you will wait a few seconds more for the results but will experience a cleaner image.

In most cases, a value of 64 will give excellent results. At the Render tab, you can see a separate value for the Viewport and Render. By default, the Viewport will always be lower than the Render. You can set the Viewport also to use 64 or more.

Keep the "Viewport Denoising" enabled to allow Blender to remove noise automatically.

7.8 Ambient Occlusion and Screen Space Reflections

If you try to add a PBR material to any surface in Eevee, it won't make reflections immediately, even with the use of a Reflection Cubemap. That is because we still have to enable the option that will consider such surfaces for rendering.

For Eevee, the option has a name of Screen Space Reflections. After you enable the feature, you will start to see reflections in Glossy Surfaces (Figure 7.18).

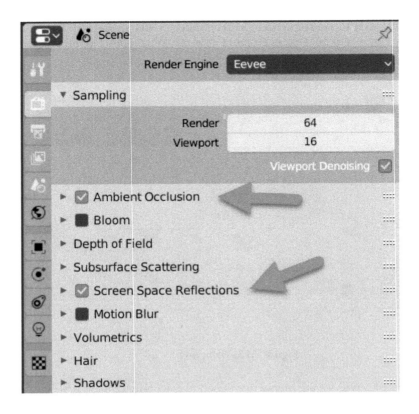

Figure 7.18 - *Screen Space Reflections and AO*

Alongside the Screen Space Reflections, you can also enable the Ambient Occlusion from the Render tab options in Eevee. The Ambient Occlusion will add what we call "Contact Shadows" that will help a lot with realism.

You will start to see the main benefit os using such effects in Eevee for realism and quality (Figure 7.19).

Figure 7.19 - *Comparing effects*

Both contact shadows and reflections will increase the realism perception of the scene.

7.9 Working with Bloom

You can also enable the Bloom effect in the Render tab for Eevee. That will add a glow effect to all surfaces that are receiving light in the render (Figure 7.20).

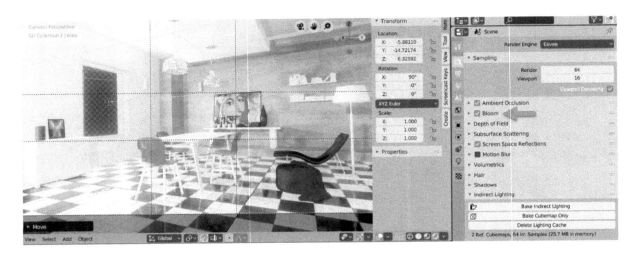

Figure 7.20 - *Bloom effect*

At the Bloom settings, you can choose aspects of the effect like intensity and distance.

7.10 Shadow quality

What if you manage to get a significant lighting effect for an interior, but your shadows still show some pixelation and irregular shapes? In Eevee, you will find a panel dedicated to controlling shadow quality. There you can choose the resolution for your shadows and enable a High Bitdepth mode (Figure 7.21).

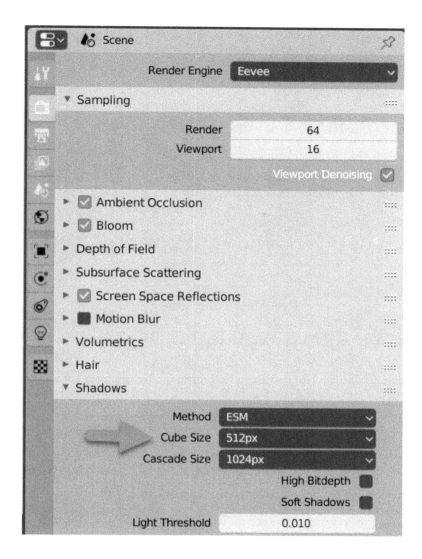

Figure 7.21 - *Shadows settings*

If you set the shadow resolution to values like 2048px for both the Cube Size and Cascate Size, you will start to see a much better result in the render. Also, enable the "High Bitdepth" to increase even more your shadow quality.

7.11 Color management adjustments

At the end of a render setup, you might still feel that you need to make final adjustments to the project like controlling the balance of black and white or changing settings like exposure.

For both Eevee and Cycles, you will find that the Colour Management options offer a wide range of tools to enhance and transform your render (Figure 7.22).

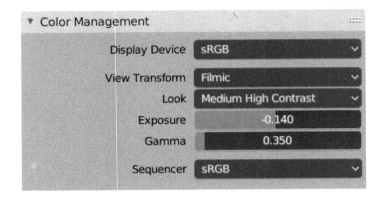

Figure 7.22 - Color management

At the Color Management options, you can control settings like:

- **Look**: Here, you will find several templates with options to choose for the contrast of your scene. For instance, you can enhance the contrast by picking the "High Contrast" option.

- **Exposure**: If you have experience with photography, the term exposure will be familiar. By changing the exposure, you will let the camera capture more or less light. The result will be a change in the overall light intensity for the scene.

- **Gamma**: With the gamma, you can control the balance of white and black in the scene.

Changing those settings could transform your render results and will depend on several factors. There is no pattern to use in architecture (Figure 7.23).

Figure 7.23 - Comparing results

You will have to play with the settings to find the best solution for a particular scene.

7.12 Camera lens for architecture

With all the settings and lights ready to render, it is time to do a final check on your camera framing and settings. In architecture, you will find that handling the camera focal distance is critical in some cases.

For instance, in interior renders where you must show a small room, you might have to change the settings of the camera to show a large area of the room.

Tip: You can easily align the camera using the CTRL+ALT+Numpad 0 keys. Use the 3D navigation shortcuts and press the keys to align the camera to your view.

Where are those settings in Blender?

If you select the camera and go to the Object Data tab at the Properties Editor, you will find the options to change your camera (Figure 7.24).

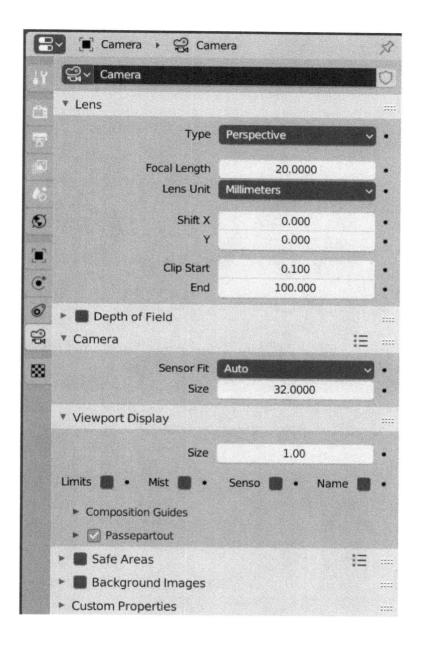

Figure 7.24 - *Camera Settings*

At the top, you can see the Focal Length settings. For instance, changing the value to something like 20mm will result in a wide lens effect (Figure 7.25).

Focal length: 55mm

Focal length: 20mm

Figure 7.25 - Wide lens for architecture

Keep in mind that using a focal length with a wide view might distort lines at the corners of your camera.

7.13 Rendering the scene

How to start a render with Eevee? You can render a scene in Blender using the F12 key or go to the **Render → Render Image** menu at the top of your interface (Figure 7.26).

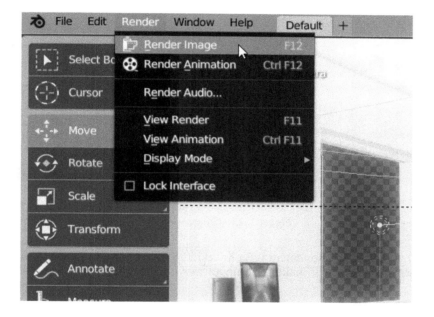

Figure 7.26 - Render Image

Blender will only render what the active camera is seeing at the moment you trigger a render.

To change your view to the camera, you can press the Numpad 0 key. You can make adjustments to the camera by selecting the border in your screen and using the transform shortcuts like the G and R keys (Figure 7.27).

Figure 7.27 - Camera border

You can even emulate a dolly movement with the camera by moving it in the local Z axis. Press the G key and the Z key twice. That will make the camera move in forward and backward if you move the mouse cursor.

The last step is to render the scene once you have the lights and camera ready. If you press F12, you will see the render results in a separate window (Figure 7.28).

210

Figure 7.28 - Render results

To save that file you have to use the **Image → Save As...** menu and choose the location you wish to save the file. At the save dialog, you can even make changes to the image format you will use to save the file.

Whats is next?

The technology behind Eevee is impressive and can give you some great results visually. But, it still lacks some level of realism for certain scenes. If you want to get the maximum realism possible with Blender for architecture, you must choose Cycles.

In the next chapter, you will learn how to prepare and work with a project for Cycles in architecture. Like we did with materials, you will also find that some settings will work on both renderers.

Chapter 8 - Rendering for architecture with Cycles

For projects that demand a high level of realism regarding rendering, you will have to choose Cycles instead of Eevee. With Cycles, you can create images using a robust algorithm called Path Tracing, which is much better for realism than the Rasterization of Eevee.

In the opposite direction of Eevee, where you had to give away some realism to speedup the render Cycles deliver exceptional images that take some time to process.

For project demanding a high level of realism, you should pick Cycles as the renderer.

In the following chapter, you will learn:

- Managing sampling for Cycles
- Applying the Denoising to renders
- Using the GPU to speed up rendering
- Manage lights for architecture
- Control HDR visibility
- Use color correction tools to enhance renders
- Prepare a test render and verify the project

8.1 Rendering with Cycles

Unlike Eevee and the real-time visualization of scenes, we have a more traditional approach with Cycles. The renderer uses an algorithm called Path Tracing to render all scenes in Blender. With Cycles, you have a few aspects of the setup process that are similar to Eevee like:

- Using an Environment Map
- Materials and Textures (PBR)
- Color correction settings

Those settings work in a very similar way on both Eevee and Cycles. For instance, once you add an HDR map to the background of your scene as an environment map, you can use it on both renderers.

How to change the renderer to Cycles? At the Render tab, you can change the renderer you want to use and set it to Cycles (Figure 8.1).

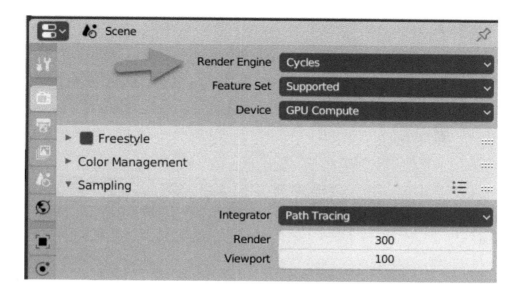

Figure 8.1 - *Choosing Cycles for rendering*

If you change the renderer to Cycles a few panels and options in Blender will change completely. For instance, you will find a lot of new options at the Render tab (Figure 8.2).

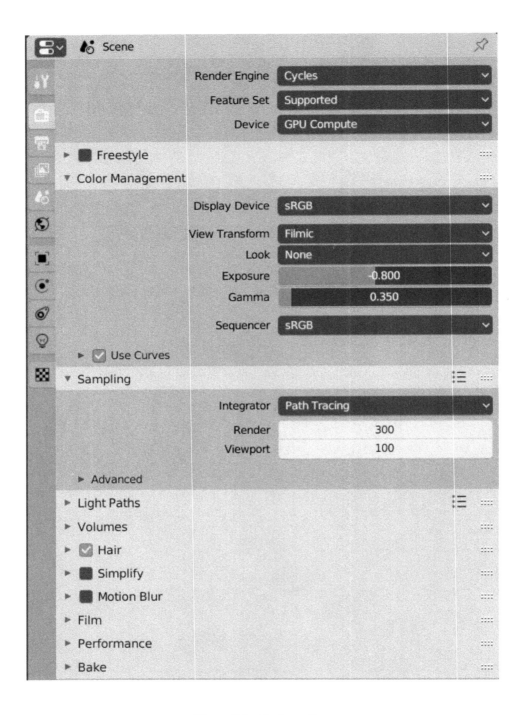

Figure 8.2 - *Cycles options*

In other panels, you will see additional controls for features like environment maps that are not available with Eevee.

8.1.1 Managing samples and denoising

To render images Cycles uses a technique called progressive refinement. It generated a low quality and noisy image, which will receive improvements over time until it reaches a clean and crispy render (Figure 8.3).

Figure 8.3 - Noisy image and final render

In theory, you can leave a project rendering in Cycles "forever" because an image will always have room for refinement. Even with a limited number of light bounces for the Path Tracing, you could leave it rendering for a long time.

You must set a limit to the processing of your render with the Sampling. At the Render tab, you will the controls for the Sampling in Cycles (Figure 8.4).

Figure 8.4 - Sampling controls

The default values of 128 and 32 for the render and viewport respectively will generate a low-quality image. What is a good value? That will depend on a lot of factors.

Usually, a value between 1500-2000 will generate a noisy free image. You can use lower values for testing purposes, but in the final render, you will eventually have to increase that number.

A tool in Blender that can help with rendering scenes in Cycles with lower values for the Sampling is the Denoising. You can enable the Denoising in the View Layer tab (Figure 8.5).

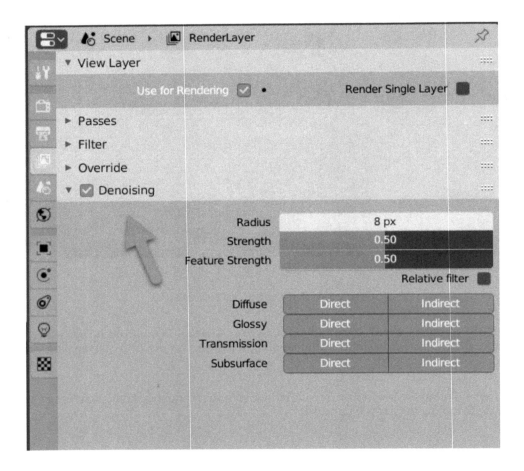

Figure 8.5 - Denoising

With the Denoising, you will be able to apply a small amount of blur to the images. As a result, you might get clean images using lower values like 200-500 for architectural renders.

8.1.2 Render times with Cycles

One of the most significant differences between Cycles and Eevee is in render times. For Eevee, you will get images in your screen in real-time and Cycles will demand a long time to process the render.

How long? That will depend on four main factors:

- The complexity of your scene (3D Models and materials)
- Sampling
- Resolution
- The computer used to render

For instance, a simple scene that doesn't have many details for rendering with a sampling of 300 and a resolution of "800 x 600" pixels will require just a few minutes to render.

However, a scene that has lots of high-poly furniture models with multiple glossy surfaces. With a sampling of 2000 and a resolution of "1920 x 1080" pixels might require a couple of hours to render. Depending on the hardware, those hours could quickly turn into days.

Info: There are several ways to speed up rendering with Cycles like adding a GPU as the main computational divide for your project.

8.2 Using a GPU to render

One of the easiest ways to speed up rendering with Cycles is to add or use a GPU to process your images. A powerful Graphical Processing Unit is a board that can handle large amounts of processing with hundreds of cores and dedicated memory.

With Cycles, you can set up the render to use your installed GPU to process the scenes, which might result in a faster render.

To enable the GPU for rendering in Cycles, you can go to the **Edit → Preferences...** menu and open the System tab (Figure 8.6).

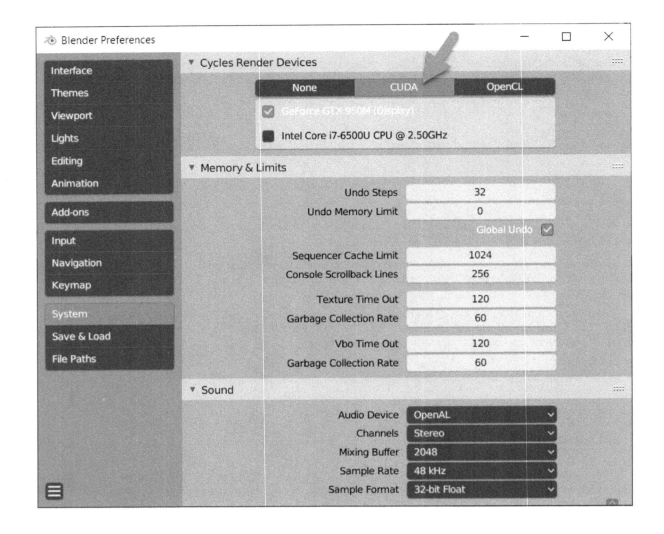

Figure 8.6 - GPU to render scenes

There you will see all compatible GPU devices in your computer, and you can enable them. At the Render tab, you also must choose the device you want to use for rendering (Figure 8.7).

Figure 8.8 - *Scene to render*

The materials and a lot of settings could remain the same.

If you are also trying to render a scene coming from Eevee, you should remove all objects related to that engine like the Irradiance Volumes and Cubemaps.

8.5 Environment maps with Cycles

From the settings that we can use with the same purpose in both Cycles and Eevee, we have Environment Maps. We can use an HDR texture in Cycles to provide more natural light from the scene and also generate reflections for glossy surfaces.

The process of adding an HDR map to the background works the same from Eevee. You have to open the World tab at the Properties Editor and add the HDR file at the Color settings (Figure 8.9).

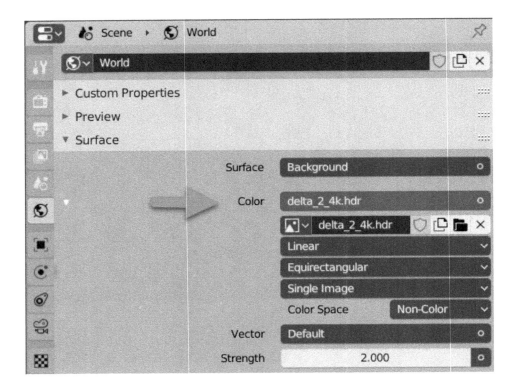

Figure 8.9 - HDR map in Cycles

The overall controls work the same for both renderers. You can set the intensity of your Environment Map using the Strength option.

8.5.1 HDR visibility with Cycles

A considerable difference here is that Cycles will display additional controls for the HDR map that are not available in Eevee. If you look below the Surface area, you will see the "Ray Visibility" options (Figure 8.10).

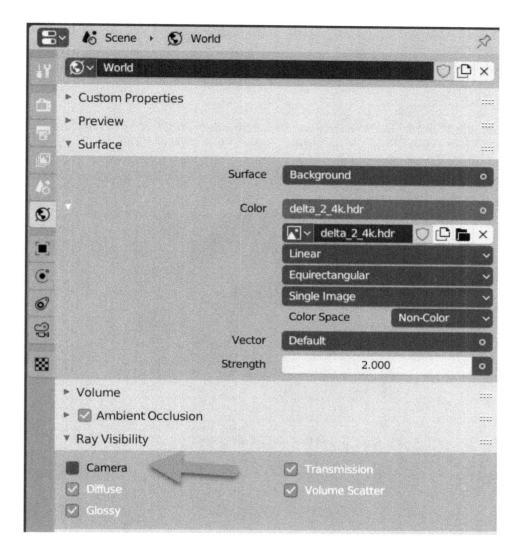

Figure 8.10 - Ray Visibility

There you can set where and how you want to view your Environment Texture. For instance, you can disable each field to have the following effect:

– **Camera**: The map won't appear in the background for the camera. It will become invisible.

– **Diffuse**: No visible light will come from the Environment Map, just retroflections.

– **Glossy**: If you don't want your map to appear on glossy surfaces, you can disable this option.

– **Transmission**: By disabling this field your HDR will not appear behind any transparent objects.

For instance, if you want to hide the HDR map from the camera, you can disable the Camera option.

8.5.2 HDR rotation

One aspect of the HDR maps that you can edit and change with both Cycles and Eevee is the rotation of that map. That is important when you have an HDR map that is also providing the Sunlight for shadows in the scene.

How to edit the HDR rotation? We can use a similar approach used for the PBR textures and tiling. We must use the Shader Editor to add a Mapping and Texture Coordinate Nodes.

First, open the Shader Editor and change the editor type to World instead of Object (Figure 8.11).

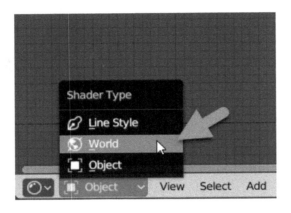

Figure 8.11 - Editor type

Once you get the Nodes for the World, you will see all the Nodes related to the Environment map. Add the following Nodes:

– Input → Texture Coordinates
– Vector → Mapping

Connect the Texture Coordinate output socket from the Generated to the Mapping, and connect the Mapping to the Environment Texture (Figure 8.12).

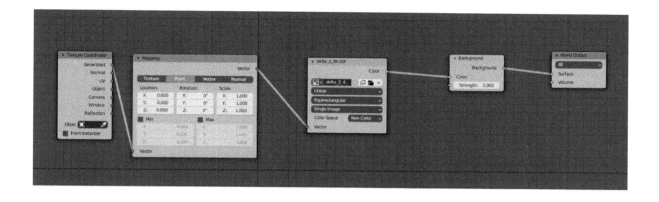

Figure 8.12 - *Nodes connections*

Now, if you change the Rotation from the Mapping, you will manipulate the rotation go your HDR map in the background.

8.6 Lights for architecture in Cycles

A topical project for architecture using Cycles will feature a similar number of light sources as Eevee. There is one aspect of the light setup that you must take special care with Cycles, which has a direct relation to the way it processes each scene with an algorithm called Path Tracing.

The way Cycles calculates each light contribution to the scene uses the Path Tracing method. It works by casting "rays" from each camera that will bounce around the scene. Once they hit a light source, the contribution of that light will appear in the render.

From that description, you can deduce:

– Small light sources will make the calculation process slower because light will bounce more until it hit the light

– You should always use large light sources to help the calculations

To put it briefly, you should always use in Cycles large size lights. The bigger, the better. Otherwise, you will have a much slower processing time for rendering.

With this in mind, we can list the top choices for lights in architecture for Cycles:

– **Environment Texture**: That is a significant source of light that will go in the background

– **Area lights**: To help with interior rendering a common technique is to use a rectangular-shaped light located at each window of a room

- **Sunlight**: If you plan to make a daylight simulation, you should use a Sun to create the primary light source for the scene

- **Objects emitting light**: In some cases, you may want to use objects to simulate surfaces that can generate light

All those lights will give you great results for an architectural visualization project with Cycles, and won't slow down the rendering.

8.6.1 Sun light with Cycles

To use a Sun in Cycles, you will find a similar process from Eevee. You can use the SHIFT+A key to add from the Light group a Sun, and with the G and R keys position and rotate the light.

If you select the light, you will be able to edit aspects of the Sun in the Properties Editor (Figure 8.13).

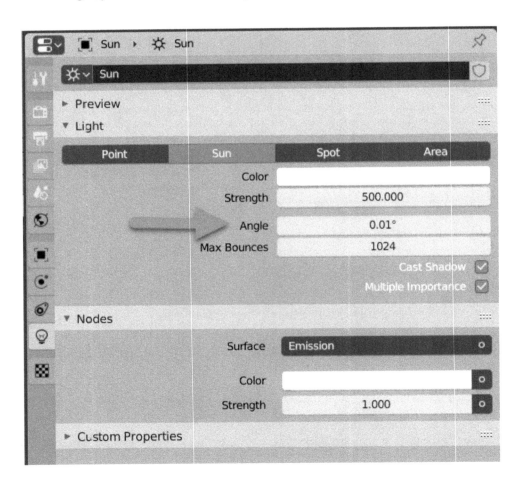

Figure 8.13 - Sun options

The number of options to change the Sun is much fewer than with Eevee. You can change aspects like:

– Strength

– Color

– Shadows

One of the essential settings regarding shadows is the Angle. That value will give you control on the shadow border. If you need a soft shadow from the Sun, you must use a high-value. For a hard edge shadow, you must use a low value like "0.01," as shown in Figure 8.14.

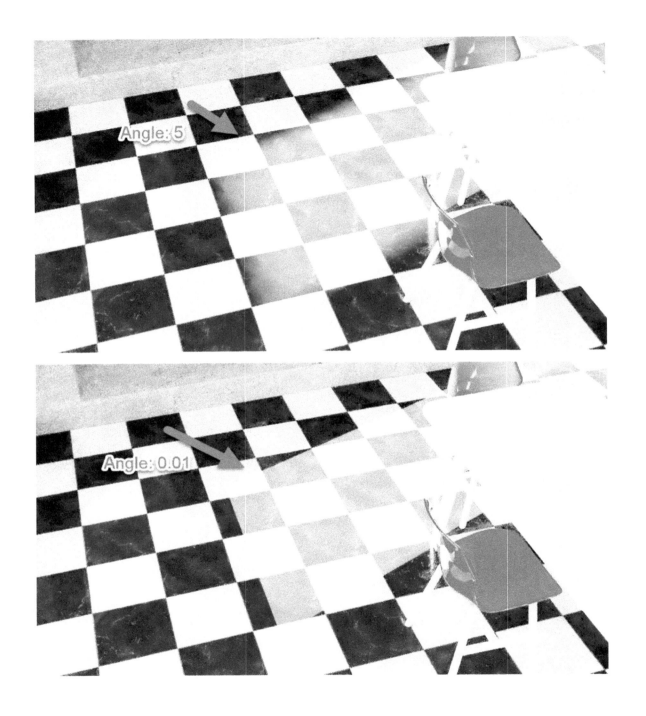

Figure 8.14 - Sun shadow

The Sun shadows are essential to define some aspects of the scene as if you have a clear sky or an overcast environment.

8.6.2 Windows and Area lights

In interior scenes, you will have to be extra careful about the lights, because they need to fill most of an enclosed space. For architectural projects, you will find that a typical project uses:

- An environment map in the background as an HDR map

- If not provided by the HDR map a Sunlight in the scene

Depending on the design of your project, you may even find that two light sources will be enough to produce good results. However, you may also experience dark spots on the scene.

That is when you will need a type of light called Area. With this light, you have a plane or rectangle that emits a constant amount of light in one direction. For interior scenes, you will have most of the light coming inside the room through windows and doors.

The trick with those lights is to add one them to each window. You will fill the space of the window with the Area light (Figure 8.15). To add even more light you can also place another one behind the camera. The same lights used for Eevee.

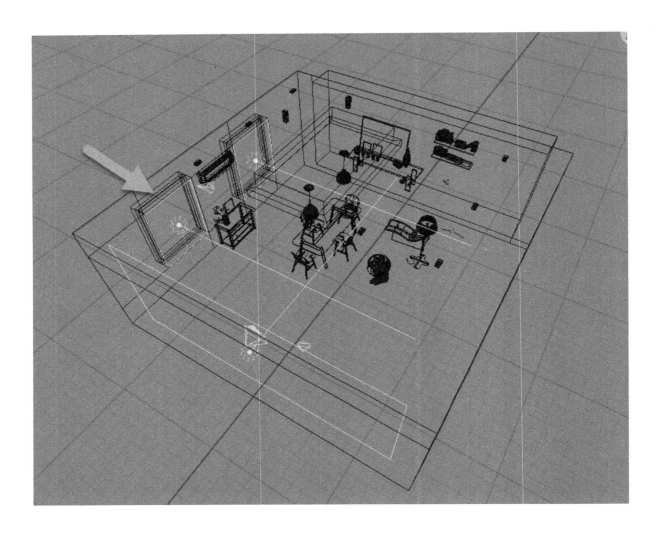

Figure 8.15 - *Window with Area light*

Once you adjust the scale of the Area, you will make sure the light is going to the interior of your scene (Figure 8.16).

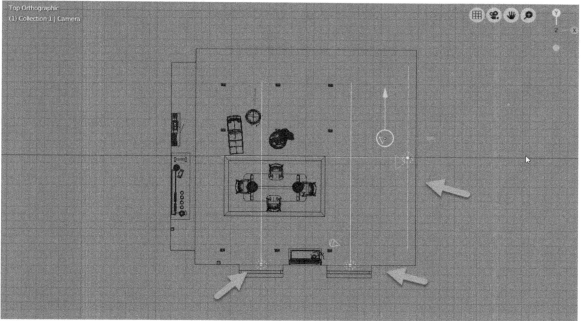

Figure 8.16 - Light direction

After you add the Area lights to the windows and doors if you think it will be necessary, you can start making adjustments to the Strength of each light to begin filling the room with light.

In some cases, you might want to use the Area lights as a location to light scape your room and speedup rendering. Like we said before regarding how Cycles works, it will solve the illumination of a scene much faster with significant light sources.

It will cast "rays" from the camera, and they will bounce until they find a light source. In closed spaces, they can bounce for a while until they get out. You may guide those rays outside the room with a Portal. The same Area light has an option called Portal, which will disable all light contribution to the scene and make the rectangle a way to guide those rays outside a closed space.

A portal is not always necessary, but if you think a scene is taking an unnecessary amount of time to render, you can add a Portal to speedup the process.

8.6.3 Using objects to emit light

Some projects may require from you the use of sources of light coming from other locations than light from Blender. You may have to use an object as the light source to simulate objects like LED panels in interiors.

You can use any object as a source of light if it has a material with the Emission shader. The process is simple and requires you to select the object and apply the material (Figure 8.12).

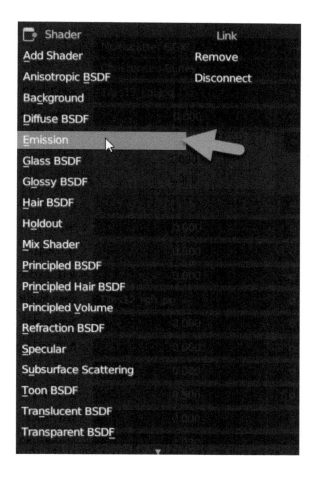

Figure 8.17 - Emission shader

At the shader, you will see options to control Strength as if it was a light source. By using this material, you will be able to create all kinds of effects for interiors.

The shader works for both Cycles and Eevee.

8.7 Contrast and exposure settings

After a few render tests, you might find your results a bit dark or with the wrong balance of blacks and whites. In that case, you can also use the Color Management options to edit and fine-tune the render in Cycles.

The process uses the same approach from Eevee, where you can change the exposure settings to make your camera receive more or fewer lights (Figure 8.18).

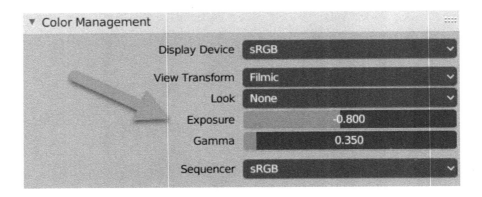

Figure 8.18 - Color management

With the Gamma settings, you can control the balance of black and white in the render. You can also use the "Look" option to pick a template for the contrast.

As a rule for Color Management, you won't find settings that apply to all projects the same way. You will have to make tests and play around with the settings. Each architectural project has a unique

8.8 Rendering the scene

After you have all the necessary elements to make a realistic illumination with Cycles, it is time to start rendering the project. Since Cycles will demand you some time to process each image, it is essential to take a few measurements to ensure you optimize that time.

Before any attempt to render your final images, you should consider making a few tests render to ensure you have:

– Materials

– Lights

– 3D Models

That is a measure to ensure you won't lose time and productivity by processing an image with potential errors.

How to set a test render? A test render should be quick and use optimal settings to make you have a great overall look at the image to start a high-quality render later.

Here are a few settings that will make your render process go a lot faster, regardless of the scene and hardware you are using:

- **Reduce your resolution**: Set the render to have something like 800 x 600 pixels in size. You can also use the scale option in the Resolution settings at the Output tab

- **Limit sampling**: For a test render, you can use a low value for sampling. A maximum of 250 with denoising should give you a good idea of how the scene looks

With those measures, you will be able to get a quick look at the image before triggering a high-resolution version. Why do you have to make a test renders? Simple, because a render from Cycles can easy take a few hours to complete. If you discover that something went wrong after a few hours, it will be hours of productivity loss.

The test renders are a measure to avoid losing time with renders that you won't be able to use.

8.8.1 Camera setup for Cycles

Before you start the final render, you will also want to make sure you have the camera at the correct location. Remember that you can use the following shortcuts and resources to improve your camera location:

- Use the CTRL+ALT+Numpap 0 keys to align the active camera to any view you have to the scene

- At the Camera, settings choose a focal length that will show your scene with all necessary details

- You can have multiple cameras in a single project, which you can make active by selecting the camera and pressing CTRL+Numpad 0

- To adjust camera framing, you can use the zoom controls. Move the camera on the local Z-axis to make a dolly movement. Press the G key and the Z key twice

The camera settings will work the same way for both Cycles and Eevee.

8.8.2 Rendering and saving the file

When you think that your scene is ready to render a high-quality image, you can start preparing to start the process. The checklist to make a high-quality render in Cycles is somehow similar to Eevee with a few extra options.

An option that you don't have with Eevee is the ability to make an image that has a transparent background. That is possible when you save the file in a format like PNG and select the color mode as RGBA.

Using an image that has a transparent background is a great help for a later composition with a sky or photo. To enable a transparent background for your renders, you must go to the Render tab and look for the Film settings. There you will see a checkbox for the "Transparent" option (Figure 8.19).

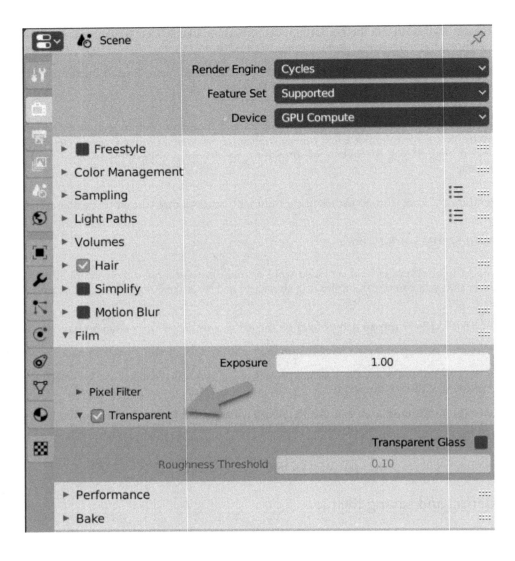

Figure 8.19 - Transparent option

Mark that option to enable Blender to create renders with a transparent background.

The next step is to ensure you have:

— A high-resolution for the image

— The correct number for the sampling

— Select the correct device to process your render (GPU or CPU)

— Enable the Denoising

If you think everything is ready, you can press the F12 key to start your rendering. Depending on your hardware, it may take a while to finish.

Tip: You can cancel the render at any time with the ESC key.

After the end of your renders, you will see the results in the output window (Figure 8.20).

Figure 8.20 - Render results

Use the **Image → Save As...** to save the results of the render to a folder on your computer.

What is next?

Where should you go from here? You know have a solid base of knowledge about Blender and architecture, and can start experimenting more about producing interactive presentations.

Blender is a great starting point for interactive presentations for architecture because it can produce accurate 3D models that you can send to Game Engines.

Another excellent opportunity to expand even more your architectural presentation skills is to dive into animation and produce clips from your future designs.

No matter what you choose to do next, you should start practicing with Blender as soon as possible to familiarise with the tools and options. In a couple of weeks, you will begin to see how practicing will make you more productive.

www.ingramcontent.com/pod-product-compliance
Lightning Source LLC
Chambersburg PA
CBHW080403060326
40689CB00019B/4118